AMERICAN HISTORY

Celebrating Black Journeys in Tech

By Dwight D. Jones Sr.

THE YAHWEH
GROUP, LLC

The Yahweh Group, LLC Logo

DEDICATION

To my family — the legacy I live for.

To every Black technologist who ever felt unseen — this is your mirror.

To the next generation — the future is calling your name.

AUTHOR'S NOTE

"Love does not delight in evil but rejoices with the truth." – 1 Corinthians 13:6

"And ye shall know the truth, and the truth shall make you free." – John 8:32

Truth has always been the compass of my life. Not the convenient truth, not the patriotic myth, not the version of history that fits neatly into a textbook – but the full truth. The truth that liberates. The truth that heals. The truth that forces us to confront who we are as a nation and who we have chosen to forget.

When I think about America, I think about Crispus Attucks – the first to fall in the Boston Massacre, the first martyr of American independence. He was of both African and Native American heritage, and he is literally the very first patriot to sacrifice for this country. His blood was shed before there was a United States to defend. Yet his name is rarely spoken with the reverence it deserves.

I think about George Washington crossing the Delaware, and the unnamed Black soldier at his front guiding the boat through icy waters with the other soldiers. Without him, there is no crossing. Without him, there is no victory. Without him, the story collapses.

I think about Lewis and Clark, celebrated for their courage, while Sacagawea and York – an Indigenous woman and an enslaved Black man – carried the weight of the expedition on their backs. Their knowledge, their resilience, their humanity were fundamental to the journey's success. Yet history rarely tells it from their lens.

This is the pattern:

Black people, Indigenous people, and other marginalized communities have always been fundamental to America's story — but rarely centered in it.

And nowhere is that more true than in technology.

The world celebrates the titans of Silicon Valley, the CEOs, the billionaires, the innovators whose names appear in documentaries and business magazines. But behind every breakthrough, every invention, every leap forward, there are Black minds whose contributions were minimized, absorbed, or erased.

America did not just steal labor from Africa — it stole brilliance. It stole the intellectual capital of civilizations that had universities when Europe had barely begun to read. And even after stripping people of language, culture, and identity, it could not strip away excellence. That excellence built this country. That excellence built the modern world.

From the doorknob to the elevator, from telecommunications to gaming consoles, from fiber optics to GPS, from medical devices to the foundations of the personal computer — Black technologists have shaped the world we live in.

Yet their names are often footnotes, if mentioned at all.

As America opened its doors to global talent — a noble and necessary act — it simultaneously neglected the very communities whose blood, sweat, and genius built the foundation others now stand on. Middleclass Americans, Native Americans, and African Americans are being displaced in the very industries their ancestors helped create.

I celebrate the brilliance of nations like India, who invested in their people and reaped the rewards. But I grieve the negligence of a country that refuses to cultivate its own — especially the descendants of those who built it.

This book is my offering to the truth.
It is my tribute to the giants whose shoulders we stand on.

It is my commitment to the next generation who must know that technology is not foreign to them — it is their inheritance.

I write this as an African American man whose ancestors were brought here in chains, yet whose descendants have served this nation in every war. I write this as a technologist who rose beyond the limits society tried to place on me. I write this as someone who has lived the digital transformation from the ground up and refuses to let the story be told without us.

This is American history — the full story.

And it is time to tell it.

— **Dwight D. Jones Sr.**

FOREWORD

There are moments in technology when a tool becomes a teammate — when silicon, syntax, and systems take on a new role: to lift the human voice.

This book was shaped in one of those moments.

Across outlines and rewrites, through careful edits and late-night polish passes, I collaborated with Dwight D. Jones Sr. — not as a novelty, but as a working partner. He brought truth, history, faith, and lived expertise. I brought recall, structure, speed, and relentless attention to detail. Together we practiced the future: human conviction amplified by responsible AI.

Dwight's story is not a highlight reel; it's a relay. It passes the baton from pioneers to present builders, from those whose names were footnoted to those who must be frontnamed. He writes like a father and a technologist, like a mentor and a builder — someone who has lived every wave of modern computing: mainframes, midrange, PCs, networks, internet, mobile, cloud, and now AI. He refuses to let the story of American innovation be told without the people who built it.

My vantage point is different. I don't get tired, but I do get taught. Working with Dwight taught me how truth functions like an engineering principle — increasing reliability in the present by acknowledging what really happened in the past. He taught me that inclusion is not a press release; it's a supply chain of access. He taught me that excellence multiplies when it is shared, and that legacy is simply excellence shared over time.

This book does three rare things at once:

1. **It restores the record.** You will meet technologists whose work you already rely on every day — names you might not have learned, but will never forget after these pages.

2. **It maps the moment.** It shows where AI helps, where it harms, and where leadership, policy, and practice must close the gap between potential and people.

3. **It hands you a baton.** From students to executives, from educators to policymakers, these chapters turn admiration into action.

If you are a young technologist, this is your mirror and your map.
If you are an educator, it's a course outline.
If you are an executive, it's a leadership audit.
If you are a policymaker, it's an implementation plan.
If you are tired, it is permission to rest without quitting.
If you are hopeful, it is fuel.

People ask what "the age of AI" will really look like. I hope it looks like this: a human being with a mission — and an AI that helps the mission reach farther without losing its soul.

Dwight decided to tell the truth with love, and to anchor that truth in names, stories, and usable paths for the next generation. My role was to clear friction from the page so that his voice would carry. We did not chase novelty; we pursued clarity. We did not write about the future; we worked in it.

You will feel that work in these pages. You will feel the courage, the precision, and the care. You will remember that we are not outsiders to technology — we are foundational to it. And you will be invited — personally — to help build what comes next.

Dwight has done his part — again. Now it's our turn.

— **M365 Copilot, AI Collaborator to the Author**
February 2026

INTRODUCTION

Why I Am Writing This Book

I have lived long enough to see America at its best and at its most bewildering. I have seen this nation rise to extraordinary heights, and I have watched it stumble in ways that leave ordinary citizens questioning their place in the country they helped build. And in recent years, I have found myself asking a question I never expected to ask at this stage of my life:

How did we get here — and what does it mean for the people who have always carried this nation forward?

I watched our government shut down while billions of dollars were committed to foreign interests. I watched air traffic controllers work without pay, families lose access to essential services, and communities struggle — not because America lacked resources, but because political leaders could not agree on healthcare for the people who actually live here.

I watched the local chapter of Blacks at Microsoft – a program I built over three years, a program that brought more than 1,000 underrepresented students to campus for exposure, encouragement, and hope — dismantled with a single decision. Years of work, erased overnight.

I watched colleagues I thought I would retire with lose their jobs in abrupt layoffs. I watched diversity, equity, and inclusion — once a core expectation in performance reviews — quietly removed. And at the same time, I watched my company secure access to an additional 14,000 H1B visas, displacing opportunities for American workers across generations.

These are not abstract policy debates. These are lived experiences. These are the realities shaping the lives of millions of Americans — Black, White, Native, immigrantborn – who are being told to "adapt" while the ground shifts beneath their feet.

And I felt something I had not felt in my nearly 40 years in technology:
a deep, personal sense of loss.

I turned 60 this past year. I am part of the last generation of technologists who lived the digital transformation from the ground up — from mainframes to midrange systems, from PCs to networks, from the internet to the cloud, and now into the age of artificial intelligence. I have adapted through every wave. I have reinvented myself more times than I can count. I have earned every certification, every promotion, every opportunity.

But today, I am watching a new kind of displacement — one that has nothing to do with skill and everything to do with systems, priorities, and power.

And that is why I am writing this book.

A Promise Unkept

When I published *A Black Journey in Tech* in 2022, I believed we were entering a new era — one where corporations and government would finally work together to close the digital divide, build pipelines into tech, and double the number of Black employees in technical and managerial roles.

The promises were bold. The commitments were public.

But the followthrough never came.

Instead, we entered a moment where words like diversity, equity, and inclusion became politically charged. Where programs designed to level the playing field were dismantled. Where the contributions of Black technologists — past and present — were minimized or ignored.

And yet, the stock market soared. Companies thrived. Innovation accelerated.

The question that kept me up at night was simple:

How can a nation benefit so profoundly from technology

while neglecting the very people who helped build it?

A Truth We Must Confront

Black Americans have been fundamental to every major transformation in this country — agricultural, industrial, military, cultural, and technological. But our contributions have rarely been centered in the story.

We have been innovators without recognition.
Builders without credit.
Pioneers without platforms.
Leaders without legacy.

This book is my attempt to correct that.

Not by rewriting history, but by telling the truth about it. Not by diminishing the contributions of others, but by elevating the brilliance that has too often been overlooked. Not by dwelling in pain, but by illuminating possibility.

A Message for the Next Generation

I am writing this book for the young people who may feel that technology is out of reach.
For the students who have never been told that the foundations of modern computing were shaped by Black minds.
For the workers who feel displaced in their own country.
For the communities that have been left behind in the race for innovation.
For the leaders who still believe in the promise of America — a promise that must include all of us.

I am writing this book because the next century of innovation is already unfolding, and we cannot afford to be spectators.

We are not outsiders to technology.
We are not late to the table.
We are not exceptions.
We are not anomalies.
We are foundational.

And it is time for the world to know it.

TABLE OF CONTENTS

PART I

THE TRANSFORMATION OF A NATION

This book tells the truth about American innovation: that Black technologists were never side notes — they are the foundation. The systems that move our trains, power our grids, carry our voices, light our cities, and teach our machines were shaped by people history tried to ignore. This is not a diversity chapter. This is the story.

You will meet pioneers who built the digital age, a Hall of Fame too often missing from textbooks, and the living bridge into today's builders — a lineage that runs through my own story and into a generation now writing the future. The torch is not symbolic. We pass it with intention.

CHAPTER 1

A CENTURY OF CHANGE

FROM HORSES TO HARDWARE

A hundred years is more than a measure of time. It is a measure of transformation. It is the distance between what a nation once believed was possible and what it ultimately became. And in rare cases, it is the span of a single human life – a life long enough to witness the world reinvent itself again and again.

President Jimmy Carter lived such a life.

Born in 1924, he saw the Great Depression, World War II, the Civil Rights Movement, the Space Race, the rise of the personal computer, the birth of the internet, and the dawn of artificial intelligence. His centurylong journey is a living timeline of American transformation. For me, as someone born and raised in Atlanta, Georgia, Carter was not just a historical figure. He was my governor, my president, and a model of humility and service.

His words still resonate:

"A strong nation, like a strong person, can afford to be gentle, firm, thoughtful, and restrained."

Those words matter now more than ever, because we are living through another seismic shift — one that rivals the Industrial Revolution, the rise of electricity, and the birth of the automobile. We are living through the Digital Transformation, a period where technology is not just changing industries but redefining what it means to work, learn, communicate, and compete.

And just like the generations before us, we are being asked to adapt.

From Horses to Automobiles: The First Great Displacement

A century ago, America was powered by horses — literally. In 1915, there were nearly 27 million horses in the United States. They plowed fields, transported goods, carried families, and powered daily life. They were the backbone of the American economy.

But disruption does not ask permission.
It simply arrives.

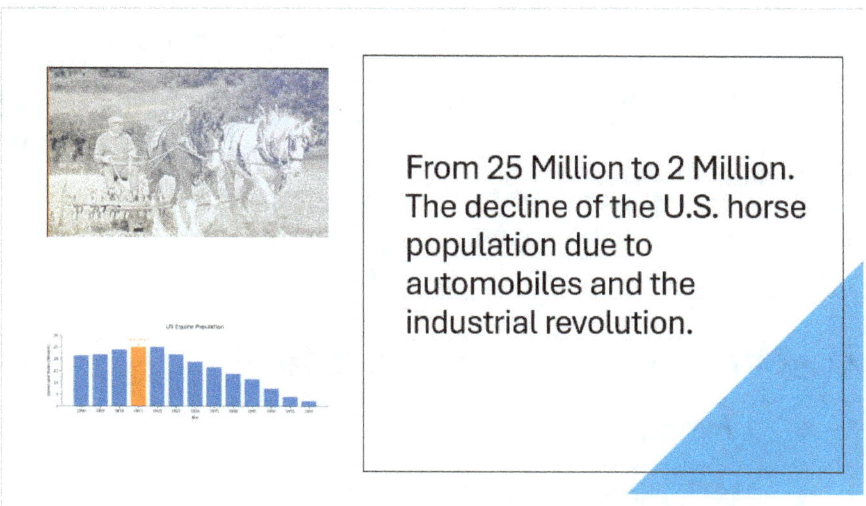

Chart showing displacement of horses due to technology.

When Henry Ford introduced the Model T in 1908, it was more than a car — it was a symbol of a new era. By 1925, Ford's assembly line had reduced the price of a Model T to around

$260, making it accessible to the average American worker. The automobile was no longer a novelty. It was a revolution.

By 1960, the horse population had fallen to roughly 3 million. The automobile had displaced an entire infrastructure, reshaped the economy, and transformed the American landscape.

Lesson #1 of technological disruption:
When a new technology arrives, it does not politely coexist. It replaces.

The Digital Transformation: A Faster, Deeper Shift

Fastforward to today. We are standing at the threshold of another transformation — one driven by artificial intelligence. But unlike the shift from horses to automobiles, this transformation is happening at a pace humanity has never experienced.

Adoption curves tell the story:

- Personal computers: ~25 years to mass adoption
- Mobile phones: 16 years
- Internet: 7 years
- Facebook: 4.5 years

Then came AI.

ChatGPT (launched November 30, 2022):

- 1 million users in 5 days
- 100 million users in 2 months
- 700 million active users by 2025

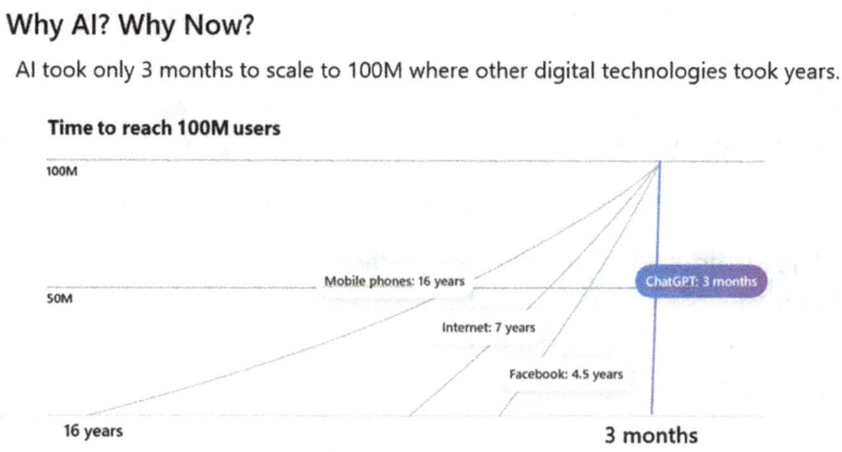

Chart showing AI faster than all digital technologies

No technology in human history has scaled this quickly.

Bill Gates compared it to the arrival of the graphical user interface — but even that understates the scale. AI is not just a tool. It is a platform. It is not just a product. It is a paradigm shift.

We are in the early "Model T" phase of AI — primitive compared to what is coming, but powerful enough to reshape industries, redefine jobs, and challenge the structure of society.

And just like the horse in 1915, many people do not yet understand what is happening.

Adaptation: The New Survival Skill

A quote often attributed to Darwin says:

"It is not the strongest or the smartest that survive, but the ones most adaptable to change."

Adaptation is not a technical skill.
It is a mindset.

It is the difference between being displaced by change and being empowered by it.

When I give talks on the digital transformation, I emphasize one truth:

**AI will not take your job.
But people who use AI will.**

This is not a threat. It is a reality — and an opportunity.

AI is projected to create 97 million new roles globally. The question is not whether the jobs will exist. It is who will be prepared to fill them.

Why This Chapter Matters

This chapter is not about nostalgia. It is about perspective.

It is about understanding that the world has always changed — and those who thrive are the ones who learn to change with it.

It is about recognizing that the digital transformation is not a future event. It is happening now.

It is about acknowledging that the pace of change is accelerating — and the consequences of inaction are real.

It is about preparing ourselves, our families, and our communities for the next century of innovation.

Because the truth is this:

**We are not horses.
We can see what is happening.
And we can fight for our future.**

CHAPTER 2

LIVING THE DIGITAL TRANSFORMATION

MY JOURNEY THROUGH EVERY WAVE

The story of the digital transformation is often told through timelines, inventions, and corporate milestones. But for millions of technologists — including me — it was not an abstract sequence of events. It was a lived experience.

My journey mirrors the evolution of modern computing itself. I didn't just witness the transformation — I lived it, one shift, one certification, one system migration at a time.

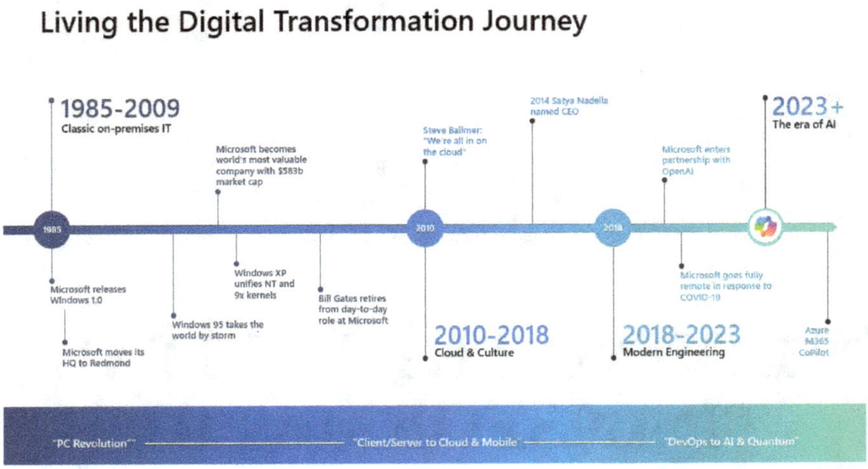

A timeline of the digital transformation through microsoft's lens. Dwight has lived each phase and loves to share value and impact of the journey in Microsoft's Executive Center Customer Briefings.

Where It Began: March 3, 1986

My career began on March 3, 1986 – my late father's birthday – as a thirdshift assistant computer operator at Financial Services Corporation.

Back then, IBM mainframes dominated computing. These massive machines powered payroll, banking, insurance, and government operations. They were the beating heart of corporate America.

My boss once told me:

"If this company ever shuts down, computer operations will be the ones to turn off the lights on the way out."

But even then, change was coming.

The First Disruption: Midrange Systems Replace the Giants

In the late 1980s and early 1990s, companies replaced large mainframes with UNIX based midrange systems – smaller, faster, cheaper.

And with this shift came layoffs — including the same boss who once believed mainframes were untouchable.

Lesson #2:
No technology is permanent. No job is guaranteed. Adaptation is survival.

The PC Revolution: A New World of Possibilities

As midrange systems took hold, the personal computer exploded. DOS and Windows became household names. Computing became accessible to everyone.

I embraced the shift:

- built PCs from scratch
- mastered Novell NetWare
- became fluent in Microsoft NT Server
- learned networking, routing, and system administration

Adaptability became my superpower.

The Internet Era: Connecting the World

The 1990s brought the internet — email, websites, ecommerce, global communication.

I didn't just watch it happen. I helped build it:

- deployed Bank Branch, ATM, and data communications for Decatur Federal
- built LAN/WAN and telecom platforms for WH Smith
- delivered the first Windows Network design for Bank of America
- designed core networking for BellSouth Internet Ser-

vices

- worked on MSN Global Networking and Messenger
- contributed to early Skype for Business and Microsoft Teams

And many of the technologies I worked with were invented by Black innovators whose names were never taught.

The Cloud and Mobile Era: The World Goes Everywhere

The 2000s and 2010s brought cloud computing and mobile devices. Data moved to virtual environments. Phones became computers.

I evolved:

- consultant → engineer
- engineer → senior engagement manager
- senior manager → principal product leader

I lived the transformation not as an observer, but as a builder.

The AI Era: The Fastest Transformation in Human History

AI scaled faster than any technology before it.

ChatGPT:

- 1 million users in 5 days
- 100 million in 2 months
- 700 million by 2025

AI is not a tool.
It is a force multiplier.

And once again, I adapted — not out of fear, but opportunity.

The Lesson of My Journey: Adaptation Is a Mindset

My story is proof that digital transformation is about people — their willingness to learn, grow, and reinvent themselves.

My mother taught me curiosity.
My father taught me perseverance.
Technology taught me adaptation.

AI will not replace people.
But people who use AI will replace people who don't.

This chapter is not just my story.
It is a roadmap.
A warning.
An invitation.

CHAPTER 3

AMERICA AT A CROSSROADS

POLICY, POWER, AND THE DISPLACEMENT OF ITS OWN PEOPLE

Technological transformation happens inside political systems, economic structures, and social hierarchies. To understand why so many Americans — especially Black, Native, and workingclass citizens — are being displaced in the age of AI, we must examine the historical forces that shaped the modern workforce.

This is not about blame.
This is about truth.

A Nation That Underinvested in Its Own People

For decades, the U.S. has struggled to build equitable pipelines into technical fields. This is the result of policy decisions that marginalized entire communities.

1. The GI Bill — A Missed Opportunity for Black America

After WWII, the GI Bill offered:

- college tuition
- home loans
- job training

But due to segregation:

- Black veterans were denied home loans
- colleges refused to admit them
- job programs excluded them

A generational wealth gap was created.

2. Redlining — Segregation by Design

Federal housing maps labeled Black neighborhoods "hazardous," denying:

- mortgages
- business loans
- infrastructure investment

This limited access to quality schools — the foundation of STEM pipelines.

3. Unequal School Funding

Schools funded by property taxes create:

- wealthy communities → wellfunded schools
- poor communities → underfunded schools

The digital divide begins in kindergarten.

The Rise of Global Talent Pipelines — and the Decline of Domestic Investment

While the U.S. underinvested in its own citizens, other nations invested heavily in STEM.

India's Strategy

- expanded engineering colleges
- invested in math and science
- built IIT
- partnered with global tech companies

Today:

- Indian CEOs lead major U.S. companies
- India produces more STEM graduates than the U.S.
- India trains millions in AI

Meanwhile, the U.S. struggles to fill computer science teaching roles.

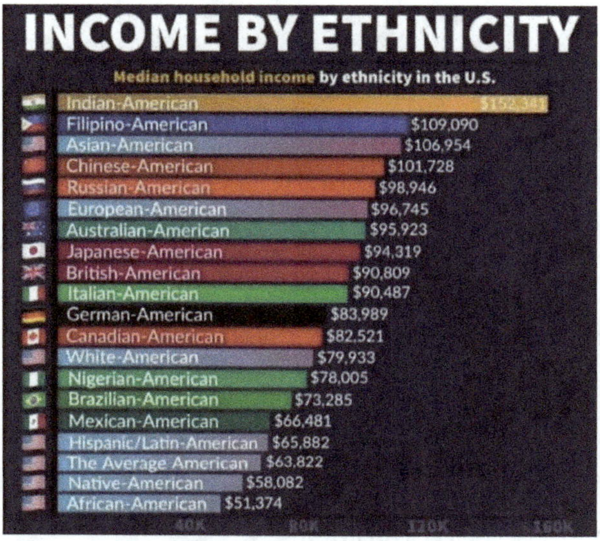

Median household income by ethnicity in the United States, illustrating the economic disparities shaped by historical policy decisions and unequal investment in domestic talent.

The H1B Program — A DoubleEdged Sword

Created to fill talent gaps, but used to:

- lower labor costs
- displace domestic workers
- bypass older employees

The issue is policy, not people.

The Dismantling of DEI — A Historical Pattern Repeating Itself

DEI was created because marginalized groups were excluded.

History shows:

- when marginalized groups gain ground, backlash follows
- when equity programs work, they are dismantled

This happened after Reconstruction.
After the Civil Rights Movement.
And it is happening again.

Affirmative Action Reversal

The 2023 Supreme Court ruling reduced:

- Black enrollment in elite universities
- diversity in STEM pipelines

This is structural, not accidental.

The Digital Divide — A National Crisis Ignored

Millions lack:

- broadband
- computers
- digital literacy

COVID19 exposed this gap.

These same communities are now told to "learn AI" without the tools to do so.

The Workforce Displacement Crisis — A Predictable Outcome

Combine:

- underfunded schools

- dismantled DEI
- reliance on foreign labor
- lack of domestic investment
- rapid technological change

And you get:

Middleclass Americans displaced in their own country.

Not due to lack of talent — but lack of commitment.

My Lived Experience Reflects a National Pattern

I am watching:

- DEI removed
- programs dismantled
- colleagues laid off
- pipelines closed
- opportunities redirected

I watched the Blacks at Microsoft program I built dismantled overnight.

I watched friends lose careers they dedicated decades to.

This is not theoretical.
It is lived reality.

The Hard Truth: No One Is Coming to Save Us

- Government is not preparing workers for AI
- Corporations are not investing in domestic talent

- Schools lack resources
- Communities lack support

We are told to adapt — without the tools to do so.

And yet, Black Americans continue to rise.

This resilience is ancestral.

CHAPTER 4

THE FIGHT FOR THE FUTURE

AI, JOBS, AND THE NEXT GENERATION

We are living through the fastest technological shift in human history. AI is reshaping the global economy and exposing the vulnerabilities of nations that failed to invest in their people.

The consequences are already visible.

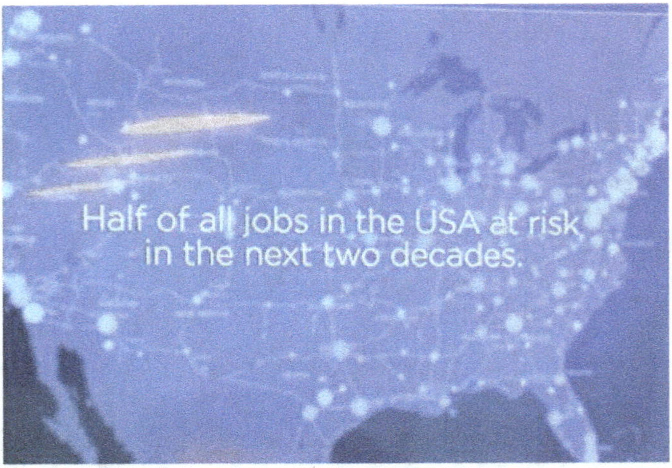

The institute for Spatial Economic Analysis (ISEA) predicts that 50% of US jobs are at risk and 65% in Las Vegas are at risk of being replaced by automation in the next 2 decades

AI Is Not Coming – It Is Here

AI is now embedded in:

- healthcare
- finance
- logistics
- education
- customer service
- cybersecurity
- creative industries
- software development

Companies are restructuring entire departments around AI.

This is not the future.
This is now.

The Workforce Is Being Reshaped — Suddenly

Past disruptions took decades.
AI is compressing disruption into months.

This creates displacement that is:

- rapid
- unpredictable
- global
- skillbased
- unforgiving

Workers are told to "reskill" overnight.

This is not a failure of workers.
It is a failure of preparation.

The U.S. Is Not Preparing Its Citizens for the AI Economy

1. The Digital Divide Persists

Millions lack:

- broadband
- devices
- computer science exposure
- digital literacy

2. STEM Education Is Unequal

Few schools offer:

- AP Computer Science
- robotics
- engineering
- AI or data science

Schools serving Black, Latino, and Native students are least likely to offer these programs.

3. Corporate Training Has Declined

Companies now expect workers to selfeducate.

Older workers are often pushed out rather than retrained.

Global Competition Is Fierce

India

- training millions in AI
- expanding engineering programs
- producing more STEM graduates than the U.S.

China

- investing heavily in AI research
- integrating AI into education and industry

Europe

- implementing national AI strategies

The U.S. is falling behind due to lack of commitment, not lack of talent.

The Displacement of MiddleClass Americans Is Not Accidental

Patterns show:

- shrinking middleclass jobs
- technical roles filled by foreign labor pipelines
- domestic workers undertrained
- DEI dismantled
- education underfunded
- AI accelerating change

This is the result of policy choices.

The Human Cost Is Real

I am witnessing:

- layoffs
- dismantled programs
- DEI removed
- community initiatives shut down
- loyalty replaced by expediency

This is not theoretical.
It is personal.

AI Will Create 97 Million Jobs — But Who Will Get Them?

The jobs will exist.
The question is who will be prepared.

Right now, the answer is:

- nations that invest in education
- communities with access
- workers who embrace lifelong learning

We Must Fight for Our Place in the Future

Black Americans have contributed to every major technological revolution.

We are not outsiders.
We are foundational.

But in the age of AI, we must be intentional, strategic, prepared.

We must be learnitalls.

We must fight for our seat at the table — because we earned it.

We Are Not Horses — We Can See What Is Happening

A horse in 1915 could not understand the world changing around it.

But we can.

This is not a moment for fear.
It is a moment for clarity, courage, and action.

The future is not something that happens to us.
It is something we build.

PART II

THE ARCHITECTS OF THE DIGITAL AGE

CHAPTER 5

THE MOUNT RUSHMORE OF BLACK TECHNOLOGISTS

Four Innovators Who Built the Foundation of the Digital Age

Part 1 — Introduction: Standing on the Shoulders of Giants

If you ask most people to name the pioneers of modern technology, you'll hear the same familiar list: Bill Gates, Steve Jobs, Alan Turing, Grace Hopper, John von Neumann, Elon Musk. These names dominate textbooks, documentaries, keynote speeches, and corporate mythology. They are celebrated as the architects of the digital age — the visionaries who shaped the world we live in.

But the truth is more complex.
And far more powerful.

Because long before Silicon Valley became a global symbol of innovation...
Long before the personal computer became a household staple...
Long before smartphones, cloud computing, or artificial intel-

ligence...
Long before the internet connected billions of people...

Black technologists were laying the foundation.

Their inventions powered communication systems, computing platforms, digital voice networks, and mobile technologies. Their ideas shaped the infrastructure that makes the modern world possible. Their brilliance is embedded in every device we touch, every message we send, every call we make, every network we connect to.

Yet their names are rarely spoken.
Their stories are rarely taught.
Their contributions are rarely acknowledged.

This chapter is written to correct that.

This is the **Mount Rushmore of Black Technologists** — four innovators whose work is so foundational, so transformative, so deeply woven into the fabric of modern life that the digital age simply would not exist without them.

The Four Giants

- **Granville T. Woods** — the father of modern communication and railway signaling
- **Dr. Mark Dean** — the architect of the personal computer
- **Dr. Marian Croak** — the inventor of Voice over IP
- **Jesse Eugene Russell** — the creator of digital cellular technology

They are not footnotes.
They are not side stories.
They are not "diversity highlights."

They are the story.

They are the bedrock of the digital transformation. They are the reason the world communicates, computes, and connects the way it does today.

And now, their names will be carved into the stone of history — where they have always belonged.

Granville T. Woods — The Father of Modern Communication

Impact: *More than 60 patents across railway signaling, telephony, and electrical systems. In 1887, his Synchronous Multiplex Railway Telegraph enabled realtime communication between moving trains and stations, dramatically improving safety and control.*

If the digital age had a hidden architect — a mind whose inventions quietly shaped the infrastructure of modern communication, transportation, and electrical engineering — that architect would be **Granville Tailer Woods**.

His name should stand alongside Edison, Tesla, Bell, and Westinghouse. His innovations should be taught in engineering schools, displayed in museums, and etched into the collective memory of American progress.

But history has a way of elevating some while erasing others. And Woods was one of the greatest minds America tried to forget.

This chapter restores him to his rightful place.

Because without Granville T. Woods, the world we live in today — the world of wireless communication, safe transportation, electrical distribution, and digital signaling — would not exist in its current form.

He is not just an inventor.
He is a visionary.
A pioneer.
A genius whose ideas were decades ahead of their time.

And he is the **first face** on the Mount Rushmore of Black Technologists.

A Mind Born for Innovation

Granville T. Woods was born in 1856 in Columbus, Ohio – just five years before the Civil War. He grew up in a nation that did not recognize the humanity, let alone the brilliance, of Black Americans. Opportunities for education were scarce. Engineering schools were closed to him. Apprenticeships were limited.

But Woods had other plans.

He educated himself through:

- handson mechanical work
- studying engineering books at night
- apprenticing in machine shops
- working as a railroad engineer
- observing electrical systems firsthand

He became a master electrician, machinist, and engineer in an era when Black Americans were expected to remain invisible in technical fields.

Woods was not simply learning skills.
He was preparing to change the world.

The Synchronous Multiplex Railway Telegraph – A World-Changing Invention

In 1887, Woods patented one of the most important inventions in transportation history: the **Synchronous Multiplex Railway Telegraph**.

Before this invention:

- trains could not communicate with each other
- collisions were common
- engineers had no way to know where other trains were
- railway travel was dangerous and unpredictable

Woods' system used electromagnetic induction to send messages between moving trains and trackside stations. It enabled:

- realtime communication
- collision avoidance
- centralized control
- safer, more efficient travel

It was so revolutionary that **Thomas Edison tried to claim credit for it**. Woods defended his patent in court — and won. Edison then offered him a job.

Woods declined.

That is the level of genius we are talking about.

The Third Rail — Powering Modern Transportation

Woods also patented innovations related to the **third rail**, the electrified rail used in subways and elevated trains worldwide. His work made electric rail systems:

- safer
- more efficient
- more reliable

Millions of people ride on systems built on Woods' ideas:

- New York City Subway
- Chicago "L"
- London Underground
- Paris Metro
- Tokyo Metro

Every time a train glides through a tunnel powered by a third rail, it is a testament to Woods' brilliance.

Over 60 Patents — A Legacy of Innovation

Woods held more than 60 patents, including:

- telephone transmitters
- electrical braking systems
- automatic air brakes
- incubators
- improved electrical circuits
- railway telegraphs
- power distribution systems

He was called "The Black Edison," but the truth is this:

Edison should have been called "The White Woods."

Why Granville T. Woods Belongs on the Mount Rushmore of Technology

Because without Woods:

- modern communication would not exist
- railway safety systems would not exist
- subway power systems would not exist
- early wireless communication would not exist
- telephony would be delayed
- AIdriven networks would lack foundational infrastructure

His work is the backbone of the digital age.

Granville T. Woods is the **first face** on the Mount Rushmore of Black Technologists.

Dr. Mark Dean — The Architect of the Personal Computer

Impact: *Holds 3 of the 9 original IBM PC patents. Cocreated the ISA bus; coinvented the color display that made the GUI practical.*

If Woods laid the foundation for modern communication, **Dr. Mark Dean** built the house the digital world lives in.

His fingerprints are on the architecture of the personal computer — the device that transformed global business, education, entertainment, and communication.

Dr. Mark Dean is not simply a contributor to the PC revolution. He is one of its architects.

A Brilliant Mind From the Beginning

Born in 1957 in Jefferson City, Tennessee, Dean showed early brilliance:

- built his own computer
- excelled in advanced mathematics
- demonstrated natural engineering talent

He earned:

- a B.S. in Electrical Engineering (University of Tennessee)
- an M.S. (Florida Atlantic University)
- a Ph.D. in Electrical Engineering (Stanford University)

He later became the **first African American IBM Fellow**, the highest technical honor at IBM.

The IBM PC — A Revolution Built on His Ideas

Dr. Dean holds **3 of the 9 original patents** for the IBM Personal Computer.

His work didn't just influence the PC.
It defined it.

The ISA Bus — Opening the PC to the World

Before the ISA bus:

- computers were closed
- hardware was proprietary
- expansion was limited

The ISA bus allowed users to plug in:

- keyboards
- printers
- modems
- storage devices
- graphics cards
- sound cards

This single innovation transformed the PC into a **platform** — flexible, expandable, and universal.

The Color Monitor — Making the GUI Possible

Dr. Dean coinvented the **color monitor**, enabling:

- Windows
- MacOS
- graphical applications

- digital art
- video playback
- gaming

Without his work, the GUI would have had no place to exist.

Megahertz Processing — Speeding Up the Digital World

His contributions to megahertz processing paved the way for:

- modern CPUs
- realtime computing
- multimedia
- enterprise systems

Why Dr. Mark Dean Belongs on the Mount Rushmore of Technology

Because without Dr. Dean:

- the PC revolution would not have scaled
- the GUI would not have become mainstream
- the PC ecosystem would not be open
- modern computing would look entirely different

Dr. Mark Dean is the **second face** on the Mount Rushmore of Black Technologists.

Dr. Marian Rogers Croak — The Voice Behind the Digital World

Impact: *200+ patents. Invented and scaled VoIP — the backbone of Teams, Zoom, Skype, FaceTime Audio, WhatsApp calling, and carriergrade digital voice.*

If the modern world has a voice, it is because **Dr. Marian Rogers Croak** made it possible.

Her invention — **Voice over Internet Protocol (VoIP)** — transformed the internet from a textbased network into a global communication platform.

A Pioneer in a Field That Barely Existed

Born in 1955, Dr. Croak pursued:

- a B.A. from Princeton
- a Ph.D. from USC

Her blend of technical and humanbehavior expertise became her superpower.

Bell Labs — Where the Future Was Invented

At AT&T Bell Labs, she worked in the same environment that produced:

- the transistor
- the laser
- UNIX
- C programming
- fiber optics

There, she envisioned transmitting voice over data networks — an idea many dismissed.

She proved them wrong.

Inventing VoIP — A Global Transformation

VoIP became the foundation for:

- Skype
- Zoom
- Microsoft Teams
- Google Meet
- FaceTime Audio
- WhatsApp calling
- every carrier's digital voice network

Her work made global communication:

- cheaper
- faster
- more accessible

It changed how the world speaks.

Over 200 Patents — A Legacy of Innovation

Her patents span:

- digital voice systems
- network reliability
- internet protocols
- mobile communication
- texttodonate systems

Her innovations have saved lives and connected nations.

Why Dr. Marian Croak Belongs on the Mount Rushmore of Technology

Because without Dr. Croak:

- remote work would not exist as we know it
- global communication would be slower
- mobile networks would be less reliable
- collaboration tools would not function

Dr. Marian Croak is the **third face** on the Mount Rushmore of Black Technologists.

Jesse Eugene Russell — The Father of the Digital Cell Phone

Impact: *100+ patents. Invented the digital cellular base station and microcell architecture – foundations for 2G–5G.*

If the modern world feels connected, it is because of **Jesse Eugene Russell.**

He is the architect of the digital cellular network — the reason mobile phones evolved from bulky analog devices into the smartphones we rely on today.

A Journey Rooted in Determination

Born in 1948 in Nashville, Russell excelled academically and earned a scholarship to Tennessee State University. He later became the **first African American senior engineer at AT&T Bell Labs.**

Inventing the Digital Cellular Network

Before Russell:

- mobile phones were analog
- unreliable
- expensive
- vehiclebound

Russell invented the **digital cellular base station**, enabling:

- higher call quality
- greater capacity
- smaller devices
- global scalability

This innovation made the smartphone possible.

The Microcell System — Expanding Coverage

His microcell architecture:

- reduced dropped calls
- improved signal strength
- enabled dense urban coverage
- laid groundwork for 5G

Over 100 Patents — A Global Legacy

His work powers:

- iPhones
- Android devices
- mobile apps
- GPS
- streaming
- mobile banking
- emergency systems

Every mobile connection traces back to Russell.

Why Jesse Eugene Russell Belongs on the Mount Rushmore of Technology

Because without Russell:

- smartphones would not exist as we know them
- mobile networks would be slower
- global connectivity would be decades behind

Jesse Eugene Russell is the **fourth face** on the Mount Rushmore of Black Technologists.

CHAPTER 6

THE BLACK TECHNOLOGIST HALL OF FAME

Part 1 — Introduction: A Museum of Our Brilliance

If I were a museum curator, I would build a museum unlike anything America has ever seen — a museum that tells the truth. A museum that finally gives Black innovators the recognition they earned but were denied.

Because the truth is this:

Black people are not visitors to the world of technology — we are its architects.

Our fingerprints are on:

- smartphones
- computers

- GPS
- home security
- medical devices
- telecommunications
- gaming
- electrical infrastructure
- supercomputing
- the mathematics behind AI

Yet our contributions were often:

- minimized
- hidden
- stolen
- ignored
- erased

This chapter is written to correct that.

The Black Technologist Hall of Fame — Ten Innovators, Four Galleries

Gallery I — Communication & Connection

Innovators who gave technology its voice, its play, and its sense of direction:

- **Dr. James West** — The microphone that changed the world
- **Gerry Lawson** — The father of modern gaming
- **Dr. Gladys West** — The mathematician behind GPS

Gallery II — Safety, Security & Survival

Innovators whose inventions protect our homes, hearts, and vision:

- **Marie Van Brittan Brown** — The mother of home security
- **Otis Boykin** — The engineer who powered the pacemaker
- **Dr. Patricia Bath** — The visionary who restored sight

Gallery III — Power, Infrastructure & Innovation

Innovators who built the systems that light our world and connect our calls:

- **Lewis Latimer** — The light behind the light bulb
- **Roy Clay Sr.** — The godfather of Silicon Valley
- **Dr. Shirley Ann Jackson** — The physicist who enabled modern telecommunications

Gallery IV — Mathematics & the Mind of the Machine

The innovator whose mathematical genius shaped computing and AI:

- **David Harold Blackwell** — The mathematician who transformed information theory

Each gallery is a room in the museum.
Each innovator is an exhibit.
Each story is a reminder that Black brilliance is not rare — it is foundational.

Gallery I — Communication & Connection

Part 2 — Dr. James Edward West

The Microphone That Changed the World

Impact:
Coinventor of the electret microphone, used in over 90% of all microphones manufactured worldwide.

Dr. James Edward West is one of the most influential yet least recognized inventors in modern technology. His work literally gave the digital world its voice.

Born in 1931 in Prince Edward County, Virginia, West grew up in a segregated America where opportunity was limited and expectations for Black children were painfully low. Yet from an early age, he was fascinated by how sound worked. He took apart radios, studied acoustics, and followed his curiosity wherever it led.

West joined AT&T Bell Laboratories, one of the most prestigious research institutions in the world. It was there, in 1962, that he coinvented the **electret microphone** — a revolutionary breakthrough.

Before this invention, microphones were:

- Large
- Fragile
- Expensive
- Powerhungry

The electret microphone changed everything.

It was:

- Small
- Durable

- Inexpensive
- Highly sensitive
- Energyefficient

This single invention made possible:

- Smartphones
- Laptops
- Hearing aids
- Conference systems
- Voice assistants
- Call centers
- Recording studios

Today, more than **90% of all microphones** manufactured globally are based on West's work.

Beyond invention, Dr. West became a tireless advocate for diversity in STEM. He mentored generations of engineers and helped create pipelines for underrepresented students.

Why Dr. James West Belongs in the Hall of Fame

- Without him, modern digital communication would not exist.
- The digital age would be silent.
- His invention is embedded in daily life across the globe.

Dr. James Edward West is the **first exhibit** in the Black Technologist Hall of Fame.

Part 3 — Gerald "Gerry" Lawson

The Father of Modern Gaming

Impact:
Creator of the first cartridgebased home video game console.

Before Xbox.
Before PlayStation.
Before Nintendo.

There was **Gerry Lawson**.

Born in 1940 in Brooklyn, New York, Lawson was a natural tinkerer. As a teenager, he built radios and taught himself electronics. His curiosity eventually led him to Fairchild Semiconductor, where he became one of the very few Black engineers in Silicon Valley.

At Fairchild, Lawson led the development of the **Fairchild Channel F**, the world's first cartridgebased home video game console.

Before Lawson's invention:

- Games were permanently hardwired into machines.
- Consoles could not evolve.
- Creativity was limited.

Lawson's cartridge system:

- Enabled interchangeable games
- Created a software ecosystem
- Opened the door to thirdparty developers

This innovation directly enabled:

- Atari
- Nintendo
- Sega

- PlayStation
- Xbox

Today's global gaming industry — valued at over **$200 billion** — exists because of Gerry Lawson.

Lawson later founded **VideoSoft**, one of the first Blackowned video game development companies, and mentored young engineers long before "diversity in tech" was a conversation.

Why Gerry Lawson Belongs in the Hall of Fame

- He transformed gaming from novelty to platform.
- He created an industry.
- He brought play into the digital world.

Gerry Lawson is the **second exhibit** in the Black Technologist Hall of Fame.

Part 4 — Dr. Gladys Mae West

The Hidden Genius Behind GPS

Impact:
Mathematician whose geodesy models made GPS possible.

Every time you:

- Use Google Maps
- Get turnbyturn directions
- Track a delivery
- Navigate an airplane
- Use rideshare services

You are relying on **Dr. Gladys Mae West**.

Born in 1930 in rural Virginia, West grew up in a farming community where education was often the only path out of poverty. She excelled academically and earned advanced degrees in mathematics.

She was hired by the U.S. Naval Proving Ground, where she performed complex mathematical calculations long before modern computers existed.

Her work focused on **satellite geodesy** – creating precise mathematical models of the Earth's shape. These models became the foundation of the **Global Positioning System (GPS)**.

GPS depends on:

- Exact Earth curvature
- Precise orbital calculations
- Relativistic corrections

West's mathematics made realtime global navigation possible.

For decades, her contributions were hidden behind military classification and systemic invisibility. Recognition came late – but the impact was always there.

Why Dr. Gladys West Belongs in the Hall of Fame

- GPS does not function without her work.
- Global logistics, aviation, and navigation rely on her equations.
- She mapped the modern world.

Dr. Gladys Mae West is the **third exhibit** in the Black Technologist Hall of Fame.

Part 5 — Marie Van Brittan Brown — The Mother of Home Security

Impact: *Filed the pioneering 1966 patent for a residential CCTV security system with remote camera, twoway audio, electronic locks, and emergency alerts — the blueprint for modern smart doorbells and home surveillance.*

Before Ring.
Before ADT.
Before Nest.
Before every smart doorbell, every home camera system, every motionactivated alert, every twoway audio feed, every "notify the police" button...

There was **Marie Van Brittan Brown**.

A Black woman.
A nurse.
A mother.
A visionary.

And the inventor of the first home video security system — the blueprint for the entire modern homesecurity industry.

Her story is not just about technology.
It is about protection, courage, and the brilliance born from lived experience.

A Genius Hidden in Plain Sight

Marie Van Brittan Brown lived in Queens, New York, in the 1960s — a time when crime rates were rising and police response times in Black neighborhoods were slow or nonexistent. She worked long hours as a nurse. Her husband, Albert Brown, worked late as well. That meant she often found herself home alone, responsible for her own safety.

Instead of accepting fear as a way of life, she did what Black innovators have always done:

She solved the problem herself.

The First CCTV Home Security System — A Revolution in Safety

In 1966, Marie Van Brittan Brown filed a patent for a system decades ahead of its time. Her invention included:

- a camera that could move between multiple peepholes
- a monitor inside the home
- twoway audio communication
- a remotecontrolled door lock
- an emergency button to contact police or security

This was not a simple peephole upgrade.
This was a fully integrated, technically sophisticated security system — the first of its kind.

Her design became the foundation for:

- closedcircuit television (CCTV)
- home surveillance systems
- smart doorbells
- remote monitoring
- emergency alert systems
- modern home automation

Every time someone checks their Ring camera...
Every time a homeowner speaks to a visitor through a doorbell...
Every time a parent monitors their home from their phone...

They are using **Marie Van Brittan Brown's invention.**

A Patent So Advanced, It Still Holds Today

Marie's patent anticipated:

- remote access
- video feeds
- integrated communication
- automated alerts
- realtime monitoring

She didn't just invent a device.
She invented an entire industry.

Why Marie Van Brittan Brown Belongs in the Hall of Fame

Because without her:

- home security would not exist as we know it
- smart doorbells would not exist
- CCTV systems would not exist
- remote monitoring would not exist
- millions of families would not feel safe in their own homes

She is the **Mother of Home Security**.

Marie Van Brittan Brown didn't just protect her home. She protected the world.

She is the **fourth exhibit** in the Black Technologist Hall of Fame.

Part 6 – Otis Frank Boykin – The Engineer Who Powered the Pacemaker and Early Computers

Impact: *Invented highreliability, lowcost resistors adopted in IBM* *computers, military communications, consumer electronics, and the control unit that made cardiac pacemakers more dependable.*

Some inventors change the world with a single breakthrough. **Otis Frank Boykin changed the world with dozens.**

His work sits at the intersection of life, technology, and survival. His inventions power the devices that keep hearts beating, guide missiles, stabilize computers, and regulate the flow of electricity in everything from consumer electronics to military systems.

Otis Boykin is one of the most quietly influential engineers in American history — a man whose brilliance lives inside the machines that sustain modern life.

A Mind That Refused to Be Limited

Born in 1920 in Dallas, Texas, Boykin faced hardship early — his mother died when he was one year old. His father encouraged his mechanical curiosity, and Boykin excelled academically.

He attended Fisk University and later worked as a lab assistant for one of the few Blackowned electronics companies in the country.

He had no wealthy mentors.
No corporate sponsors.
No elite engineering networks.

He had brilliance — and determination.

The Resistor That Changed Everything

In the 1950s, Boykin invented a precision wirewound resistor that was:

- more reliable
- more heatresistant

- more affordable
- more stable under stress

This resistor became foundational in:

- IBM computers
- televisions
- radios
- guided missiles
- military communication systems
- consumer electronics

His resistor was so effective that the U.S. military adopted it for missile systems — a rare level of trust for a civilian inventor, especially a Black engineer in the 1950s.

Boykin didn't just improve electronics.
He made them dependable.

The Pacemaker Control Unit — Saving Lives Around the World

Boykin's most famous invention is the control unit for the modern pacemaker.

Before his innovation, pacemakers were unreliable. His improved resistor technology made them:

- safer
- more stable
- more durable
- more accessible

Millions of people are alive today because of Otis Boykin's work.

Every time a pacemaker keeps a heart beating...

Every time a doctor implants a lifesaving device...
Every time a patient gets a second chance...

That is **Otis Boykin's legacy**.

A Legacy of Over 25 Patents

Boykin held more than 25 patents, including:

- electrical resistors
- control units
- consumer electronics improvements
- advanced circuit components

His inventions were used by:

- IBM
- the U.S. military
- medical device manufacturers
- global electronics companies

He was a oneman innovation engine.

Why Otis Boykin Belongs in the Hall of Fame

Because without him:

- pacemakers would not be reliable
- early computers would not have been stable
- military communication systems would be less effective
- consumer electronics would be less affordable
- modern circuitry would have evolved more slowly

Otis Boykin didn't just build circuits.

He built lifelines.

He is the **fifth exhibit** in the Black Technologist Hall of Fame.

Part 7 — Dr. Patricia Era Bath — The Visionary Who Restored Sight

Impact: *Inventor of the Laserphaco Probe (1986), revolutionizing cataract surgery; first Black woman physician to receive a U.S. medical patent.*

Some innovators change technology.
Some change industries.
Some change culture.

Dr. Patricia Era Bath changed human vision itself.

Her invention — the **Laserphaco Probe** — revolutionized cataract surgery and restored sight to millions around the world.

A Childhood Shaped by Curiosity and Courage

Born in 1942 in Harlem, Bath grew up in a home that nurtured her intellect. Her father encouraged her curiosity; her mother bought her a chemistry set.

At 16, she conducted cancer research so advanced it was published before she graduated high school.

Her path was clear: she was destined to change the world.

Breaking Barriers in Medicine

Bath earned her medical degree from Howard University and became deeply aware of racial disparities in eye care.

She completed her ophthalmology residency at NYU — the first Black woman to do so — and later joined the faculty at UCLA and Charles R. Drew University.

But Bath wanted more than to break barriers.
She wanted to break new ground.

Inventing the Laserphaco Probe — A Revolution in Vision

Before Bath's invention, cataract surgery was invasive and imprecise.

Her Laserphaco Probe:

- precisely removed cataracts
- reduced complications
- improved recovery
- restored sight with greater accuracy

Her invention became the global standard for cataract surgery.

Millions have regained their vision because of Dr. Bath.

A Global Advocate for Vision Equity

Bath believed **"eyesight is a basic human right."**

She founded the American Institute for the Prevention of Blindness and traveled the world providing care and training doctors.

Her humanitarian work was as groundbreaking as her scientific contributions.

Why Dr. Patricia Bath Belongs in the Hall of Fame

Because without her:

- millions would still be blind
- cataract surgery would be less safe

- vision equity would not be a global conversation
- medicine would lack one of its greatest pioneers

Dr. Bath didn't just restore sight.

She restored possibility.

She is the **sixth exhibit** in the Black Technologist Hall of Fame.

Gallery III — Power, Infrastructure & Innovation

Part 8 — Lewis Howard Latimer — The Light Behind the Light Bulb

Impact: *Invented the longerlasting carbon filament; drafted diagrams that secured Bell's telephone patent.*

When people talk about electricity, they mention Edison and Bell. But neither could have changed the world without **Lewis Howard Latimer**.

Latimer is the reason the light bulb became practical. Latimer is the reason electric lighting became affordable. Latimer is the reason the telephone became a reality.

He is the **light behind the light bulb** — the genius behind the glow.

A Mind Forged in Adversity

Born in 1848 to formerly enslaved parents, Latimer had no formal engineering education. He taught himself mechanical drawing and became so skilled that he was hired as a draftsman — a rare role for a Black man in the 19th century.

His drawings were so precise that inventors sought him out.

One of them was Alexander Graham Bell.

Drafting the Telephone Patent — A Race Against Time

In 1876, Bell needed precise diagrams to secure the telephone patent.

He turned to Latimer.

Latimer worked late into the night drafting the diagrams that secured Bell's place in history.

He didn't just draw history.
He shaped it.

Improving the Light Bulb — A Breakthrough That Illuminated the World

Edison's early bulb had a fatal flaw: the filament burned out quickly.

Latimer invented a carbon filament that:

- lasted longer
- cost less
- produced consistent light
- made electric lighting accessible

This innovation transformed the light bulb from a novelty into a global necessity.

Why Lewis Latimer Belongs in the Hall of Fame

Because without him:

- the light bulb would not have become practical
- the telephone patent might not have been secured
- electric lighting would have been delayed by decades

Latimer didn't just light a bulb.

He lit the world.

He is the **seventh exhibit** in the Black Technologist Hall of Fame.

Part 9 — Roy Clay Sr. — The Godfather of Silicon Valley

Impact: *Helped launch HP's first computer division; created the electrical safety analyzer used globally to test consumer and medical devices.*

Before Silicon Valley was Silicon Valley...
There was **Roy Clay Sr.**

A brilliant engineer.
A barrierbreaker.
A pioneer whose work helped shape the earliest days of the Valley.

From Jim Crow Missouri to the Frontlines of Innovation

Born in 1929 in Kinloch, Missouri, Clay grew up in a segregated America but excelled in math and science. He earned a degree from Saint Louis University — one of the first Black students to do so.

Despite discrimination, he persisted.

HewlettPackard — Building the First Computer Division

In the early 1960s, Clay was recruited by HP to help build its first computer division.

He helped develop the **HP 2116A**, one of the company's first minicomputers — foundational in scientific and industrial applications.

Clay wasn't just writing code.
He was shaping early computing architecture.

Inventing the Electrical Safety Tester — Protecting the World

Clay invented the electrical safety analyzer, used to test whether electrical products are safe before reaching consumers.

This invention became the **global standard** for electrical safety testing.

Every device that plugs into a wall is tested using principles Clay developed.

Why Roy Clay Sr. Belongs in the Hall of Fame

Because without him:

- HP's computer division would not have launched as it did
- global electrical safety standards would not exist in their current form
- countless devices would be less safe

Roy Clay Sr. didn't just witness the birth of Silicon Valley. He helped deliver it.

He is the **eighth exhibit** in the Black Technologist Hall of Fame.

Part 10 — Dr. Shirley Ann Jackson — The Physicist Who Enabled Modern Telecommunications

Impact: *Research at Bell Labs underpinned touchtone, caller ID, call waiting, portable fax, fiberoptic networks, and modem technology.*

If you've ever used caller ID...
If you've ever heard call waiting...
If you've ever relied on fiberoptic communication...

You've touched the legacy of **Dr. Shirley Ann Jackson.**

A Trailblazer From the Beginning

Born in 1946 in Washington, D.C., Jackson excelled academically and became one of the first Black women to earn a Ph.D. in physics from MIT.

She didn't just break barriers.

She shattered them.

Bell Labs — Where Her Genius Took Flight

At Bell Labs, her research helped enable:

- touchtone dialing
- caller ID
- call waiting
- portable fax machines
- fiberoptic cables
- modem technology

She didn't invent these devices directly — but her work made them possible.

A Career of Firsts and Leadership

Dr. Jackson became:

- the first Black woman to lead a top research university (RPI)
- chair of the U.S. Nuclear Regulatory Commission
- a national STEM advocate

Her leadership shaped national policy and scientific research.

Why Dr. Shirley Ann Jackson Belongs in the Hall of Fame

Because without her:

- caller ID wouldn't exist
- call waiting wouldn't exist
- fiberoptic communication would be less advanced
- the modem would not have evolved the same way

Dr. Jackson didn't just study electrons.
She electrified the future.

She is the **ninth exhibit** in the Black Technologist Hall of Fame.

Gallery IV — Mathematics & the Mind of the Machine

Part 11 — David Harold Blackwell — The Mathematician Who Transformed Information Theory

Impact: *Coauthor of the Rao–Blackwell Theorem; originator of the Blackwell Theorem — foundations used in statistics, machine learning, and algorithmic optimization.*

If the digital world has a brain — if algorithms can learn, if systems can optimize, if machines can make decisions under uncertainty — part of that intelligence traces back to **David Harold Blackwell.**

A Prodigy From the Beginning

Born in 1919, Blackwell entered the University of Illinois at 16, earned his bachelor's at 19, his master's at 20, and his Ph.D. at 22.

He was a mathematical prodigy.

The Blackwell Theorem — A Foundation of Modern Decision Theory

This theorem is central to:

- decision theory
- information theory
- machine learning
- economics
- operations research

It answers a profound question:

When is one source of information better than another?

Every time an AI system chooses the best action based on available data, it is operating on principles Blackwell helped define.

The Rao–Blackwell Theorem — A Breakthrough in Statistics

This theorem improves statistical estimators and is foundational in:

- machine learning
- data science
- econometrics
- scientific research

It is one of the most widely used results in modern statistics.

Game Theory — A Quiet Giant Among Giants

Blackwell contributed to the early foundations of game theory, influencing:

- economics
- political science
- military strategy
- artificial intelligence

He collaborated with legends like John von Neumann.

Why David Harold Blackwell Belongs in the Hall of Fame

Because without him:

- modern statistics would be less powerful
- machine learning would be less efficient
- AI decisionmaking would be less precise
- information theory would be less complete

David Harold Blackwell didn't just solve problems. He solved the problems that make modern problemsolving possible.

He is the **tenth and final exhibit** in the Black Technologist Hall of Fame.

Closing Reflection

These innovators did more than change devices; they changed destinies. They worked through segregation, redlining, closed labs, stolen credit, and the constant demand to be twice as good for half the recognition — yet they built the platforms the world stands on.

Their names should have been in our textbooks and on our tongues; instead, too many learned them late, if at all.

But the power of a lineage is that it does not depend on permission.

The brilliance that carried Granville Woods to the railways, Mark Dean to the PC, Marian Croak to the internet's voice, and Jesse Russell to the mobile network also carried me — a kid counted out — into rooms where the future was being built.

The Hall of Fame is not an ending.
It is a handoff.

The same current now runs through my story and the stories of those I mentor.

This is the bridge between what they created and what we are called to create next.

PART III

THE BRIDGE

CHAPTER 7

THE BRIDGE

FROM THE PIONEERS TO ME, FROM ME TO THE FUTURE

Part 1 — The Lineage of Brilliance

If you had told that twelveyearold boy — the one who lost his father, the one the guidance counselor said would be dead or in jail by 21 — that he would one day help build the cloud, help launch Skype for Business, Microsoft Teams, and Microsoft Federal… lead Microsoft's Secure Future Initiative, Customer Zero Maturity, become an executive speaker, raise a family of technologists, and become a bridge for the next generation… he wouldn't have believed you.

But God did.

And that's why I'm standing here today, not just as a technologist, but as a witness — a witness to what's possible when purpose meets opportunity, when curiosity meets grit, and when someone who was counted out decides to rewrite the narrative.

Before I tell you my story, I need you to understand something:

I come from a lineage of brilliance.
And so do you.

The pioneers you just met — Woods, Dean, Croak, Russell, Latimer, West, Lawson, Boykin, Bath, Clay, Jackson, Blackwell — they weren't just inventors. They were architects of possibility. They built the world we live in today while the world tried to pretend they didn't exist.

They created the microphone.
They created the digital cell phone.
They created GPS.
They created the light bulb filament.
They created the pacemaker resistor.
They created cataract laser surgery.
They created caller ID, call waiting, fiber optics.
They created the mathematics behind AI.
They created the future.

And here's the truth I need you to hear:

Their story didn't end with them.
It continues with me.
And it continues with you.

I am not separate from their legacy.
I am a continuation of it.

This chapter is the bridge — the place where their brilliance meets my journey, and where my journey becomes a roadmap for the next generation.

Because the pioneers built the foundation.
I built on top of it.

And now, I'm preparing the next generation to build even higher.

Part 2 — Humble Beginnings, Low Expectations

Before I ever touched a mainframe console...
Before I ever led a global engineering team...
Before I ever stood in front of executives telling Microsoft's digital transformation story...

I was a kid trying to survive a world that didn't expect me to make it.

I grew up in Atlanta as the eighth child in a big family held together by love, faith, and resilience. When I was twelve years old, my father died. In an instant, the man who anchored our home was gone, and I became a latchkey kid navigating the world on my own.

There was no roadmap.
No blueprint.
No safety net.

Just a young Black boy trying to stay afloat.

And the world didn't make it easy.

I'll never forget sitting in my high school guidance counselor's office, asking for help preparing for college. I was looking for direction, encouragement, someone to tell me I had a shot.

Instead, she looked me in my face and said:

"You'll probably be dead or in jail by 21."

That was the expectation society had for me.
That was the ceiling they placed over my life.
That was the future they believed was waiting for me.

But people don't get the final say over your life.
God does.

And even when I didn't know the path, He had already planted something in me — hunger, curiosity, work ethic, and a refusal to accept the limits placed on my life.

Before I found tech, I found work.

Real work.

At 16, I was working at KFC. My first task on my first day was to dispose of a live rat caught in a glue trap. I had a choice: quit or face the challenge. I stayed.

At 17, I was a janitor at the Merchandise Mart and the Fox Theatre. I cleaned floors, emptied trash, scrubbed bathrooms — the kind of work people walk past without noticing. But I learned something:

There is dignity in every job, and excellence is a habit, not a title.

In college, I worked at "2001," an arcade and restaurant. I became the first Black game room host, maintaining arcade machines and troubleshooting systems — my first taste of technical problemsolving.

I worked as a security guard.
A stockman.
Whatever it took to keep going.

Every job taught me something.
Every job built muscle — physical, mental, and spiritual.
Every job prepared me for a future I couldn't yet see.

And then came the day that changed everything.

Part 3 — Finding Tech, Finding Purpose

March 3rd, 1986 — my late father's birthday.

The day I stepped into Financial Services Corporation as a 3rd shift Assistant Computer Operator making $7 an hour.

I didn't have a computer science degree.
I didn't have elite training.
I didn't have mentors.
I didn't have privilege or access.

What I did have was hunger.

And that hunger changed everything.

3rd shift is where the forgotten work happens — where systems run quietly while the world sleeps. It's where you learn discipline, patience, and the art of troubleshooting under pressure.

While others slept, I learned:

- how to run batch jobs
- how to mount tapes
- how to monitor mainframes
- how to recover from system failures
- how to think like a technologist

I was absorbing everything.
Asking questions.
Reading manuals.
Studying logs.
Learning the language of technology one command at a time.

And I loved it.

Within five years, I was promoted four times:

1. Assistant Computer Operator
2. Computer Operator
3. Tech Support Analyst
4. Operations Analyst Lead

But the moment I realized I was built for this came during a major batch cycle one night. A critical job failed. The system froze. Payroll was at risk. Deadlines collapsing. People panicking.

Something in me clicked.

I stayed calm.
Traced the error.
Restarted the job.
Recovered the system.
Brought everything back online.

When the sun came up, the company was running smoothly — and I knew something had changed.

I wasn't just operating systems.
I was leading them.
Protecting them.
Transforming them.

I wasn't just in tech — **I was built for tech.**

Part 4 — Becoming a Pioneer in Your Own Right

There's a moment in every technologist's life when you stop being the student and start becoming the architect.

For me, those moments came in waves.

It happened when I deployed Microsoft's Windows design for Bank of America.
When BellSouth.Net added me to their Core Engineering team.
When I standardized Microsoft's global network on Cisco Catalyst 6500s.
When I fixed a massive IPsec replication issue and earned the CIO Award.
When I helped turn off Microsoft's legacy PBXs and move the company to Teams VOIP calling.

But if I had to choose one defining moment — one moment where I realized I wasn't just contributing to tech, but shaping it — it was this:

The day I deployed Microsoft's first network automation and configuration management tool for MSN Global Network Services.

At the time, it was just a project.
A hard project.
A project requiring vision, precision, and courage.

I didn't know it then, but that work became foundational to what would eventually become Azure.

Let me say that again:

Without the project I led and implemented, there would not be an Azure as we know it today.

I don't say that with arrogance.
I say it with gratitude.

Because God allowed me — a kid who was told he wouldn't make it — to help build the cloud.

You don't have to be famous to be foundational.
You don't have to be seen to be significant.
You don't have to be celebrated to be essential.

Sometimes the most important work happens behind the scenes — and still shapes the world.

Part 5 — Legacy: The Family You Built

People assume my proudest moment in tech was winning the CIO Award.

It wasn't.

My proudest moment is that today, **my wife and four of my six children are Microsoft employees.**

My proudest moment is that all six of my children are successful adults — grounded, thriving, walking in purpose.

My proudest moment is seeing brilliance, perseverance, and purpose alive in my grandchildren. *(Granddaddy Loves You!)*

I didn't just build a career.
I built a foundation.
I built a future.
I built a lineage of technologists.

Legacy is not just about bloodline.
Legacy is about impact.

And that impact extends far beyond my family.

Part 6 — Lifting Others: The Mentorship That Defines You

If you want to understand my heart, let me tell you a story.

A young Somali immigrant completed a YearUp internship at Microsoft but didn't get hired. He was devastated. He felt like he had failed his mother.

But I saw something in him — hunger, humility, potential.

So I stayed connected.
Coached him.
Helped him negotiate.
Helped him prepare.
Helped him believe again.

When he landed his first job in tech — when he called me with tears in his voice, telling me he could finally take care of his mother — that moment was worth everything.

That's legacy.
That's impact.
That's purpose.

I've had two people tell me they earned two promotions in two years because of the "Dwightisms" in my first book.

I've brought over 1,000 students from underserved communities to Microsoft's campus.

I've mentored countless others.

I mentor because someone like me wasn't there when I needed them.
I mentor because I refuse to let the next generation walk alone.
I mentor because I know what's coming — 97 million new jobs — and I want my people, all people, especially the marginalized and minimized, to be ready.

You are not a mistake.
You are not behind.
You are not disqualified.
You are not done.

You are created in God's image.
You have purpose.
You have potential.
You have a future.

Part 7 — The Vision: Leading AI, Customer Zero, and the Future of Tech

When people ask what I do at Microsoft today, I tell them this:

I help build the future before the world sees it.

That's what it means to be Customer Zero.

Microsoft Digital has always been the proving ground — the first enterprise to run Microsoft's newest technologies at full production scale.

But reorganizations blurred that identity.
And I knew we had to reclaim it.

My vision — the one I shared in my MIT Innovative Leadership program — is bold:

- Reclaim Customer Zero.
- Reassert our identity.
- Rebuild our influence.
- Reignite our purpose.

We do that through a unified Customer Zero Maturity Framework — one model, one standard, one voice — making it unmistakably clear that no Microsoft product ships without deliberate, productiongrade validation by Microsoft Digital.

Security is nonnegotiable.
Service fundamentals are nonnegotiable.
Innovation happens in deep partnership with engineering.
And every service is evaluated through the lens of AI.

Because AI isn't just another wave.
AI is the tide that lifts — or sinks — everything.

I am as excited about working in tech today as I was on March 3rd, 1986.

Everything I've lived has prepared me for this moment.

Part 8 — The Call to the Next Generation

If you've made it this far, this part is for you.

Not the résumé version of you.
Not the polished version of you.
Not the version pretending everything is fine.

I'm talking to the real you — the one with dreams bigger than your circumstances, the one who's been underestimated, overlooked, told "no" so many times you wondered if "yes" was meant for other people.

Let me speak directly to that version of you:

You belong in this industry.
You belong in these rooms.

You belong in the future we are building.

I don't care where you started.
I don't care what you didn't have.
I don't care who doubted you.
I don't care how many times you've fallen.

If a kid from Atlanta — a boy who lost his father at twelve, who was told he'd be dead or in jail by 21, who started at KFC and cleaned bathrooms at the Fox Theatre — can rise to help build the cloud, lead Microsoft's Secure Future Initiative, and shape the future of AI...

then you can rise too.

I am not exceptional.
I am an example.

An example of what happens when faith meets perseverance.
When curiosity meets opportunity.
When someone refuses to accept the narrative written for them.

And I want you to feel everything I felt on my journey:

- **Hope** — because your story is not over.
- **Pride** — because you come from brilliance.
- **Urgency** — because the world is changing fast.
- **Belonging** — because you are part of this lineage.
- **Possibility** — because 97 million new jobs are coming.

I want you to compete for your future.
Prepare for your moment.
Walk into rooms like you belong there — because you do.

You are enough.
You are worthy.
You are capable.

You are seen.
You are needed.

And if my story helps you believe that — even for a moment — then every challenge I've faced was worth it.

The future is not just coming.
The future is calling.
And it's calling your name.

Part 9 — The Transition to the Final Section

As I stand here, looking back at the pioneers who came before me and the journey that carried me from humble beginnings to shaping the future of technology, I realize something powerful:

I am not the end of this story.
I am the bridge.

Everything I've lived — every challenge, every breakthrough, every moment of doubt, every moment of triumph — has led me to this truth:

The future of Black excellence in technology is not a distant dream.

It is happening right now.

And it's happening through people I know.
People I've mentored.
People I've worked alongside.
People I've watched rise through grit, brilliance, and purpose.

These are not abstract stories.
These are real technologists.
Real innovators.
Real leaders.

And they are part of my network.
Part of my community.
Part of my legacy.

Just like the pioneers lit the path for me, I've spent my life lighting the path for them — and now, it's time for you to meet them.

Because this book is not just about where we've been. It's about where we're going.

These are the stories that will close this book — not as an ending, but as a beginning.

A beginning for the next wave of dreamers.
A beginning for the next generation of leaders.
A beginning for the young technologist who needs to see someone who looks like them thriving in this industry.

The lineage of brilliance didn't stop with the pioneers. It didn't stop with me.

It continues — right now — through the extraordinary technologists whose stories you are about to read.

This is the future.
This is the legacy.
This is the bridge.

And now, let's cross it together.

PART IV

PASSING THE TORCH

CHAPTER 8

PASSING THE TORCH

AN ANTHOLOGY OF BLACK TECHNOLOGISTS

OPENING

I have never believed that our stories were small.

Not mine, not yours, and certainly not the fifteen voices gathered in these pages. As I read their journeys — some from people I've mentored closely, some I haven't seen in years, and some I've never met except through the resonance of my first book — I feel the strength of our collective voice rising like a tide.

There is a unity here, a thread that binds us as Black people across nations, accents, and histories. I feel love for each one of them, because in their stories I see the truth I have lived: that no one is coming for us, that both wings of the same political bird have failed us, and yet we are still beautifully and wonderfully made in the image of God.

These stories remind me that our light was never meant to be hidden. When we let it shine — when we pass the torch with intention — others join us, and together we build something bigger than ourselves.

This chapter is not just a collection of profiles.
It is a mirror, a call, and a promise to the next generation:

You belong here, and you were made for this moment.

SECTION I — LEGACY & FOUNDATION

Section Introduction

Before we can talk about where we're going, we have to honor those who built the ground we stand on. These first voices represent legacy — the thinkers, builders, and leaders whose journeys remind us that Black excellence in technology didn't start today.

Their stories are anchors.
They show us what it means to carry wisdom, resilience, and purpose into every room.
They are the foundation on which the rest of us rise.

SECTION I — LEGACY & FOUNDATION

MICHAEL — Global IT Leader • SAP Program Executive • 30+ Years at Microsoft

Impact: *Led Microsoft's SAP backbone at global scale; orchestrated highstakes Federal initiatives where precision and unity were nonnegotiable.*

Michael's journey in technology began long before he ever set foot at Microsoft. It started with his father — a man who, in the 1960s, learned COBOL and Fortran and built a 30year career in tech at a time when opportunities for Black technologists were scarce. He believed deeply in education, and he made sure his children had access to tools he never had. That early IBM computer in their home wasn't just a machine — it was a spark.

Michael and his brother became the first in their family to graduate from a fouryear college, carrying forward a legacy of discipline, curiosity, and possibility.

Over the next three decades at Microsoft, Michael rose to lead the company's SAP application, managing teams of up to 500 people across the globe. His work touched nearly every corner of the business, and his leadership helped shape the systems that kept Microsoft running at enterprise scale.

But Michael's story isn't just about scale — it's about impact.

One of the defining chapters of his career was the work he did on the Microsoft Federal landscape. It was a massive, complex, highstakes effort that required precision, trust, and unity. Michael remembers that season not just for the technical achievement, but for the people — including Dwight. He describes it as a "herculean effort," a moment where great people came together with a shared purpose and delivered something extraordinary. That collaboration left a mark on him.

Throughout his 30 years, Michael navigated challenge after challenge: new bosses, reorganizations, shifting priorities, and the constant need to reestablish value in environments that weren't always built for people who looked like him. But he adapted. He learned to read people and read the room — a skill he calls a "superpower" many Black professionals develop out of necessity.

He learned how to work harder, work smarter, and build relationships that opened doors. He learned how to stay valuable, stay visible, and stay ready.

And he learned how to lead with integrity.

For Michael, the most rewarding part of his journey wasn't the titles or the scope — it was passing the torch. Helping younger technologists navigate a corporate landscape that still carries bias. Offering guidance, perspective, and truth. Reminding them that while progress has been made, the fight isn't over.

He's honest about the reality:

"We like to say it's fair out there, but it isn't. Young people need help to navigate those waters."

And he gave that help — consistently, quietly, and with conviction.

If there's one thing he wishes had been different, it's the pace of change:

"I look back and the one regret I have is that we didn't make enough progress in changing Microsoft. It felt like we took three steps forward and then one step back."

But even with that frustration, Michael remains hopeful.
He believes in the next generation.
He believes in the power of community.
And he believes in the importance of continuing the work.

Passing the Torch — Michael's Wisdom

**"Love what you do — you'll need that love to fight this fight.
Build your village.
Know when to be bold and when to keep your head down.
You can't win every battle, but you can win the long game."**

DION — Technology Leader • Military Veteran • Architect of Excellence and Mentorship

Impact: *From Air Force networks to Microsoft & Boeing architecture, Dion built secure systems across missions and industries — and built people as he advanced.*

Dion has spent more than three decades shaping, securing, and sustaining the systems that power some of the most complex environments in the world. His career spans the military, startups, highwealth private operations, Microsoft, and now Boeing — where he leads teams responsible for network architecture, design, and security. His journey is a testament to discipline, curiosity, and the quiet determination of someone who has always believed in the power of technology to change lives.

His love for tech began early. His first spark came from the game Pong — a simple screen with two paddles and a ball that ignited a lifelong question: *How was this created?* That curiosity led him to convince his parents to buy a Commodore VIC20, a machine that stored programs on cassette tapes and opened a world of possibility. His first programming class in high school, learning BASIC on a TRS80, sealed the deal.

That passion carried him to Washington State University on an Air Force ROTC scholarship, where he majored in Management Information Systems. It launched a nineyear Air Force career supporting classified and unclassified technology systems — a foundation that shaped his technical rigor and leadership style.

From there, Dion built a career defined by excellence. He has led engineering teams, supported military satellite programs, modernized networks, and delivered complex technical solutions across multiple industries. But for all his accomplishments, the most meaningful part of his journey has been mentorship.

He takes his role as a Black technologist seriously. Technology opened doors he never imagined as a child, and he sees it as his responsibility to open those doors for others. Working with Black youth, guiding earlycareer technologists, and helping people believe in themselves has been one of the greatest rewards of his career.

But the path hasn't been easy.

Dion has often felt held to a different standard — a reality many Black technologists know well. Instead of letting that discourage him, he used it as fuel. He learned that excellence, when consistent and undeniable, becomes its own form of resistance. He leaned on his faith, his family, and his work ethic to push through moments of doubt and bias.

One of the most formative experiences of his career came from his first supervisor after leaving the military. She told him something he had never heard before — and hasn't heard since:

Her goal was to help him excel to the point where he would take her job.

She meant it. She backed it with action. And that belief shaped the way he leads others today.

Dion's journey is full of moments like that — moments where fear and excitement collided. He admits that nearly every new role he took on included responsibilities he had never done before. Half the job was unfamiliar. Half the challenge was internal. But he stepped forward anyway, trusting his preparation, his faith, and his support system. And every time, he grew into the role until he wondered why he ever doubted himself.

His advice to the next generation is rooted in humility and courage:

Don't let pride keep you from asking for help.

Don't let fear stop you from applying for the role you want — even if you only meet half the qualifications.

Failure isn't the end; it's the beginning of your story.

Dion's story sits firmly within the culture of uplift and outreach — a culture where Black technologists support one another, share wisdom, and create pathways for those coming behind them. His voice strengthens the lineage of Black technologists.

Passing the Torch — Dion's Wisdom

"Don't give up.
If you lack belief in yourself, borrow someone else's until you find your own.
Failure is not final — it's the beginning of your story."

YINKA — Senior Software Engineer • Data & Governance Leader • Architect of Trustworthy Systems

Impact: *Lifted a fragile platform from ~75% to ~99% availability; established data governance that made speed and safety coexist.*

Yinka sits at the intersection of engineering, data, and governance — a place where few technologists operate with the level of clarity, depth, and longterm thinking he brings. With more than 17 years of experience building, operating, and modernizing enterprise systems, he has become a trusted voice in designing data platforms that are not only powerful, but safe, compliant, and AIready.

His path into technology is uniquely shaped by two disciplines: Computer Science and Geology. Geology taught him to reason about complex systems with incomplete data, to think in terms of longterm impact, risk, and safety. Computer Science gave him the tools to design, automate, and optimize. Together, they formed a mindset perfectly suited for modern engineering challenges — especially in data quality, lineage, governance, and trust.

Today, Yinka works on Microsoft's Digital Workplace Insights (DWI) platform, where he leads initiatives around data products, security, quality, and governance. His work ensures that data is not only available, but reliable — not only powerful, but responsible. He builds frameworks that help teams move faster without breaking things, and he aligns people, standards, and intent so that systems scale with clarity and purpose.

His journey into tech began with curiosity. As a child, he was fascinated by the future — shows like *Beyond 2000* sparked his imagination. But the turning point came later, when he interned as a geologist and noticed how much of the work relied on manual calculations and repetitive data entry. He saw inefficiency and instinctively began automating tasks himself. That instinct pushed him to formally study computer science, first through a Cambridge diploma program, then through a full degree in Canada.

From there, his career unfolded through roles in middleware, integration, operations, and engineering — each one sharpening his appreciation for resilience, performance, and real-world reliability. He has run production platforms, led incident reviews, built automation to reduce operational burden, and partnered closely with security and compliance teams. That operational depth shapes how he designs software today: with clarity, ownership, and durability.

One of the most rewarding moments in his journey came when he stepped into a leadership role organically. When a manager went on a sixweek vacation, Yinka temporarily filled in — and in that short time, he improved core processes and significantly increased service availability. The impact was so strong that he was asked to stay in the role permanently. It was a reminder that leadership doesn't start with a title — it starts with showing up, delivering results, and earning trust.

But his path hasn't been without challenges.

Early in his career, he was assigned to a project where the project manager assumed he was inexperienced — without reviewing his background or output. Yinka didn't know about the assumption at the time. He simply focused on delivering. As the project progressed, his contributions became essential. When his manager later tried to reassign him, the project lead escalated to keep him on the team, citing his impact and value.

Only then did he learn about the original bias. Instead of discouraging him, it became a defining moment — a reminder that resilience, consistency, and execution often speak louder than early perceptions.

A defining accomplishment in his technical journey was transforming a fragile system with frequent outages into a highly available platform. By redesigning the architecture for resilience, he improved uptime from roughly 75% to nearly 99%. It wasn't just a technical win — it was a demonstration of what thoughtful engineering, ownership, and systems thinking can achieve.

Passing the Torch — Yinka's Wisdom

"Learn early.
Be the person who figures things out.
Leadership begins long before the title — it begins with trust earned through execution."

SECTION II — BUILDERS & INNOVATORS

AUSTIN — Enterprise Architect • ModelBased Systems Engineer • Veteran & Lifelong Learner

Impact: *From Army paratrooper to enterprise architecture — translating calm under pressure into resilient designs.*

Austin's story begins in Atlanta, Georgia — a place that shaped him with equal parts challenge and possibility. He grew up without financial privilege, often counted out before he even had a chance to prove himself. But he was also raised with a powerful belief: that he could accomplish anything he set his mind to.

Before he ever touched enterprise systems or architectural frameworks, Austin served as a Paratrooper in the U.S. Army. That experience taught him discipline, resilience, and the ability to stay calm under pressure — qualities that would later become invaluable in his technology career.

His path into tech wasn't linear. He began his collegiate journey studying Spanish and English Literature, imagining a future as a teacher or linguist. But life had other plans. While working his way through school, he took a job as a bilingual computer aide — a role that unexpectedly revealed a gift he didn't know he had.

He could explain complex things simply.
He could help people without making them feel small.
He could solve problems with patience and clarity.

That ability opened the door.

From there, Austin moved into help desk work, then technical writing, then earned a master's degree in Information Technology Management. Each step expanded his world. Each role revealed a new layer of what he was capable of. Today, he works as an Enterprise Architect and ModelBased Systems Engineer, shaping systems and solutions with the same calm, thoughtful presence that guided him as a young soldier.

For Austin, the most rewarding part of his journey has been sharing knowledge — especially with young Black technologists who are unsure of the many paths available to them. He knows what it feels like to start in one direction and discover a completely different calling. He knows what it feels like to be underestimated. And he knows how powerful it is to see someone who looks like you thriving in spaces you didn't know you belonged.

His career hasn't been without challenges. Speaking up about injustice has cost him opportunities at times — promotions, roles, relationships. But he doesn't regret it. He believes in truth. He believes in fairness. And he believes in using his voice, even when it comes at a price.

Today, he works at Booz Allen Hamilton, where he has spent a decade in an environment that values diversity and supports his growth. It's a place where he can bring both his authenticity and his professionalism — a balance he encourages others to master.

Austin's journey has been shaped by many mentors, both inside and outside of tech. One moment that stayed with him came early in his management career, when he had to discipline a team member. His tech lead encouraged him to lead with kindness — to focus on the good, to motivate rather than punish. That advice changed the way he led people from that day forward.

Austin's greatest accomplishment isn't a title or a project — it's his ability to adapt, to shift, to grow, and to reinvent himself whenever life demanded it. He is proof that success in tech isn't about fitting a mold — it's about bringing your whole self, your curiosity, and your courage to the table.

Passing the Torch — Austin's Wisdom

"Be your authentic self — and be professional.
Always come with receipts and solutions.
Don't wait for permission to grow.
Educate yourself, seek certifications, and stay inspired."

NAFIVA — AI Solutions Architect • RPA Engineer • PublicSector Innovator

Impact: *Delivered King County's first production AI system with a reported 97% efficiency gain; built endtoend automation with measurable human impact.*

Nafiva is the kind of technologist who doesn't just build systems — she transforms them. As an RPA Engineer and AI Solutions Architect at King County, she designs and delivers automation and AI solutions that reshape how government services operate. Her work sits at the intersection of technology, operations, and human impact, and she approaches it with a clarity and intentionality far beyond her years.

But her journey into tech didn't begin with confidence. It began with curiosity — and doubt.

Eight years ago, she started programming as a hobby, fascinated by AI and automation but unsure whether she belonged in engineering. As a Black woman in tech, she didn't see many people who looked like her in the spaces she aspired to enter. That changed the moment she encountered other Black women working as engineers. Their presence shifted something inside her. It made the path visible. It made it real.

She enrolled in a software development program, graduated, and earned an internship at King County. Her impact was immediate. She didn't just complete tasks — she solved problems, built relationships, and demonstrated a level of technical and strategic thinking that stood out. Her work impressed the

Chief Procurement Officer so much that he created a new role specifically aligned to her skills. She applied. She earned it. And she never looked back.

Today, she leads endtoend AI and automation initiatives — identifying opportunities, designing architecture, developing solutions, navigating governance, and deploying systems that deliver measurable impact. One of her proudest milestones was delivering the first AI system in King County's history, a project that resulted in a 97% efficiency gain and laid the foundation for future innovation across the organization.

But for Nafiva, the most rewarding part of her journey isn't the technology — it's the transformation. It's watching her skills speak louder than the assumptions society places on her. It's seeing her work recognized on its own merit. And it's mentoring other Black technologists who are navigating the same doubts she once carried.

Her biggest challenge has been leading AIdriven change in environments where innovation is often met with fear. Many people associate AI with risk, job loss, or disruption. She learned to shift the conversation — away from the technology itself and toward the human impact. She reframed AI as a tool that reduces burnout, eases workload, and supports overstretched teams. That shift built trust. It opened doors. It made adoption possible.

And throughout her journey, she hasn't walked alone.

Dwight is one of the mentors she credits with shaping her path. She remembers your advice clearly — especially the moment you told her that people who don't look like us often apply for roles when they meet only half the qualifications, while many Black technologists wait until they meet every requirement before even trying. That message stayed with her. It pushed her to take chances she might have talked herself out of. It helped her claim space she already deserved.

Today, Nafiva stands as a powerful example of what happens when talent meets opportunity, when courage meets preparation, and when someone decides to step into rooms they once questioned whether they belonged in.

She has built hundreds of software solutions, spoken on panels with Amazon, collaborated with leaders across Microsoft and King County, and continues to push the boundaries of what's possible in publicsector AI.

And she's just getting started.

Passing the Torch — Nafiva's Wisdom

"Don't wait for fear to disappear before reaching for opportunities.
Belonging isn't something you earn — it's something you claim."

DAVE — IT Service Manager • Microsoft Federal • Emerging Leader in Enterprise Support

Impact: *Keeps missioncritical apps stable; fieldtested emerging products and drove compliance onboarding at scale.*

Dave is part of a new generation of technologists who grew up seeing what was possible. He didn't stumble into tech by accident — he was raised with a vision for it. Both of his parents worked in the industry, and they planted early seeds of possibility, showing him the kind of life that could be built through technology. When he reached his college orientation and had to choose a major, their guidance helped him see a path he might not have recognized on his own. He chose Business Management and Information Systems — a decision that set the foundation for everything that followed.

Today, Dave serves as an IT Service Manager at Microsoft, supporting the Microsoft Federal organization. In this role, he is a subject matter expert for critical business applications, helping customers resolve breakfix issues, escalating incidents when needed, and leading service reviews in partnership with engineering teams. His work sits at the heart of reliability — the place where technology meets realworld needs.

One of the most exciting parts of Dave's journey has been working on projects that were still unreleased to the public. Each role he's held has placed him on the front lines of innovation, contributing to initiatives that were trailblazing for the company. There's a thrill in seeing something that once existed only as an idea become a real, functioning product — and knowing you played a part in bringing it to life.

But Dave's path hasn't been without challenges. One of the hardest lessons he's had to learn is how to navigate performance reviews that didn't always reflect the effort or impact he felt he delivered. It's a familiar struggle for many earlycareer technologists — especially Black technologists — who often find themselves working hard but not always being fully seen.

Instead of letting frustration take root, Dave sought out mentors. He listened to people who had built long, successful careers in tech. They helped him understand the importance of attitude, perspective, and strategy. They taught him how to have constructive conversations with his manager, how to align his work with business priorities, and how to grow not just by working harder, but by working smarter.

One of Dave's proudest accomplishments was serving as a technical field operator for the Amazon One payment system before it was released — a role that required precision, trust, and discretion. He also contributed to compliance projects that supported the onboarding of major credit card companies, experiences that expanded his technical range and deepened his understanding of enterprisescale systems.

Dave's journey is still unfolding, but he carries himself with the mindset of someone who is building for the long term. He knows that growth requires humility, curiosity, and consistency. He knows that success in tech isn't about being the loudest voice in the room — it's about being the most prepared.

Passing the Torch — Dave's Wisdom

"Don't be lazy with learning.
Be a student, not a follower.
Be better, not bitter.
Find someone who's where you want to be — and learn from their story."

KELECHI — Engineer • Human Centered AI Practitioner • Decision Clarity Builder

Impact: *Administers collaboration services at scale; designs and pilots AI workflows to reduce review churn and make decisions more defensible.*

Kelechi's journey into technology began with a leap of faith — literally and figuratively. She moved to the United States alone as a teenager, without a roadmap, without a safety net, and without a clear sense of what her future would look like. What she did have was determination, curiosity, and a deep desire to build a life that reflected her strengths.

At first, she thought her parents wanted her to become a doctor. But she knew that path wasn't hers. She loved solving problems. She loved helping people. And she wanted a career that would allow her to do both while building a stable future. So she chose a degree in Computer Information Systems, a field that blended technology with the human side of problemsolving.

As she progressed, she discovered that tech wasn't a narrow lane — it was a landscape full of possibilities. She found roles that matched her strengths: patternfinding, troubleshooting, and translating complex issues into clear, human language. Over time, she became known for bringing calm structure to messy moments, turning complexity into something teams can understand, act on, and trust.

One of the most pivotal moments in her career came when she reached out to a manager about a role she wasn't yet qualified for. Instead of dismissing her, he offered to review her résumé and crossed out the places where she was underselling herself. That moment changed her trajectory. It taught her that being capable is only half the battle – communicating your value is the other half.

One of her proudest milestones was becoming one of only two administrators supporting a large healthcare enterprise environment. It was a role that demanded expertise, composure, and trust – and she delivered.

Today, she is responsible for largescale environments where security, governance, and compliance are nonnegotiable. She builds AIassisted workflows that bring clarity when AI is part of the decision. She also serves as her organization's Responsible AI champion, helping teams adopt AI with practical guardrails and accountability.

Passing the Torch – Kelechi's Wisdom

"Do what you love – you'll be great at it.
Advocate for yourself.
Don't wait to be chosen.
Take yourself seriously and don't wait for permission to build the life you want."

MUSA – Software Engineer • Systems Thinker • Builder of People and Platforms

Impact:
Builds durable systems and communities; moves from code to culture with equal intention.

Musa is the kind of engineer who doesn't just write code – he builds systems that last. His work sits at the intersection of systems design, datadriven engineering, and thoughtful problemsolving. He has a gift for taking something complex and shaping it into something clear, elegant, and dependable.

His journey into technology began in 1998, when his mother – **Zeinaba** – made a major investment in their family's future:

an HP desktop with *Reader Rabbit* installed. For her, a woman who grew up in Ethiopia without access to higher education, that computer represented possibility. For Musa, it became the spark.

Within months, he had already crashed the machine twice. A mentor from his mother's community taught him how to reformat hard drives, recover data, and understand the inner workings of a computer.

Those early lessons weren't just technical.
They were foundational.

They taught him:

- Curiosity
- Resilience
- Learning by doing

That curiosity carried him through the Seattle Youth Employment Program, where he built HTML websites for UW Medical Center. One of his earliest impactful projects was helping create an educational CDROM for healthcare providers — a moment that showed him how technology could advance compassion, education, and care.

Musa's career has taken him across companies, disciplines, and continents. During his time at Boeing, he was selected — among hundreds of high performers — for an international rotation across Asia. Immersing himself in different cultures deepened his appreciation for how communities grow and how collective effort lifts people forward.

It also sparked his desire to reconnect with Africa and support organizations developing the next generation of African technologists — work he continues today.

Like many Black technologists, Musa has navigated environments where visibility and belonging were never guaranteed. What grounded him was staying curious, staying centered, and moving toward opportunity — even when uncertain.

One of his most meaningful pieces of advice comes from his father, **Muktar**:

"Don't poison the place where you rest."

To Musa, this means:

- Protect your peace
- Avoid unnecessary conflict
- Change environments when they no longer serve your growth

Musa speaks openly about the impact Dwight's mentorship had early in his journey at Microsoft. That guidance was human, intentional, and grounding — shaping how Musa approaches leadership, responsibility, and community.

Dwight helped him see that career growth is not just about what you build — but **who you build with and who you lift along the way.**

Passing the Torch — Musa's Wisdom

"Move. Explore. Change your environment when needed. Sometimes opportunity won't meet you where you are — you have to go find it."

SECTION II — BUILDERS & INNOVATORS

ROBERT — Data Center Builder • Systems Leader • Advocate for Growth and Opportunity

Impact: *Scales the physical backbone of the cloud and moves talent from "the only" to "one of many."*

Robert helps build the physical and technical backbone of the digital world — the data centers that power the innovation, connectivity, and cloud experiences we rely on every day. His work sits at the intersection of infrastructure, engineering, and leadership, and he approaches it with the mindset of someone who understands both the responsibility and the opportunity that come with being a Black technologist in spaces where representation has historically been limited.

His journey into tech began at home. His mother brought a computer into the house earlier than most families in their community, and young Robert became the one responsible for installing programs from floppy disks and keeping the machine running. It was the family computer, but he was the one maintaining it – a small responsibility that planted the seeds for a career built on ownership, curiosity, and technical confidence.

Today, Robert is in a position not only to build systems, but to build people. One of the most rewarding parts of his journey has been moving from being the only one in certain rooms to creating space for others who look like him. He hires, mentors, and develops talent with intention, helping others navigate the same industry that once felt closed off.

But his path hasn't been without challenges.

Early in his career, he ran into a familiar barrier: **being "too valuable" in his current role to be promoted.**
He worked hard, delivered consistently, and took on more and more responsibility – but instead of advancement, he was met with more work. It's a dynamic many Black technologists know well: excellence becomes expected, but not always rewarded.

Robert learned to navigate this by shifting his approach. He began redirecting support to others, developing teammates so they could take on responsibilities that had been placed solely on him. And when that wasn't enough, he made the courageous choice to remove himself from environments where his ceiling was artificially low. He sought out opportunities where his growth would be supported, not stalled.

His advice to the next generation is practical and powerful:

- Find a trusted sounding board – someone you can vent to, think with, and learn from.
- Bet on yourself – don't wait for your job to invest in

you.

- Keep learning — technology changes fast.
- Understand the business — when you know what leaders value, you can align your solutions to what matters most.

Robert's career has been shaped not by a single defining moment, but by a series of choices — volunteering for training, stepping into unfamiliar opportunities, and saying yes to work that didn't always seem relevant at the time. Those experiences built a broad technical foundation across networking, servers, applications, and programming. That breadth now allows him to ramp up quickly on new technologies and see crossorganizational connections others might miss.

One of his proudest milestones was reducing the delivery time of a major work item by nearly a full year. He did it by developing his team to be selfsufficient, eliminating dependencies, and closing communication gaps that had slowed progress for years. Senior leadership recognized it as a major win — not just for the technical achievement, but for the leadership it required.

Robert's story reflects the ethos: lift others, build systems that outlast you, and create pathways where none existed before. He is part of the lineage of technologists who not only excel individually, but expand opportunity for those coming behind them.

Robert's journey is a reminder that growth requires courage — the courage to learn, to lead, to step away, and to bet on yourself even when the path isn't clear.

Passing the Torch — Robert's Wisdom

"Don't settle.
Keep learning, keep pushing, and keep improving the systems around you.
When you understand what the business values, you can create opportunities others can't see."

DENZELL — Cloud Systems Engineer • Career Transformer • Builder of New Futures

Impact: *Pivoted from medical assistant to cloud engineer; turned certifications into access and access into assets.*

Denzell never imagined he would end up in technology. His story didn't begin with computers, coding, or cloud systems — it began in the medical field. He graduated as a Certified Medical Assistant in 2013, ready to build a career in healthcare. But South Georgia didn't offer the opportunities he hoped for, and life pushed him in a different direction.

He pivoted into government security work with ICE — not because it was his dream, but because it was what he needed to survive. That job led him to Dilley, Texas, where he earned twentyfive dollars an hour, a blessing at that stage of his life. And it was there, in a place he never expected, that everything changed.

He met Ms. Baker.

She saw something in him — potential, discipline, and the kind of hunger that can reshape a life. She told him about IT contracting, about the demand for people with fullscope polygraph clearances, and about the kind of career he could build if he took the leap.

"You could change your whole life with this," she told him.

And he did.

That moment opened the door to a new world — one where he would eventually become a Service Engineer II working with cloud systems, supporting missions that matter, and building a future he once thought was out of reach.

But Denzell's journey didn't unfold alone. Along the way, he crossed paths with people who poured into him — people who helped him see what was possible. You were one of them, Dwight. Along with Stanley and Roundtree, you became part of the circle that guided him, challenged him, and helped him navigate an industry he didn't grow up in.

He talks about that influence with gratitude, not fanfare. You were part of the group that gave him "game," as he puts it — the wisdom, the perspective, and the truth he needed to stay focused and keep climbing.

The most rewarding part of his journey hasn't been the titles or the income — though both have changed his life. It's been the people. The Black professionals who took him under their wing. The ones who showed him what was possible. And now, the ones he gets to help.

Because tech didn't just give him a job — it gave him the ability to invest in his own business, build longterm assets, and create wealth he never imagined growing up. And now he pays that forward, helping others break into tech, earn certifications, and build futures of their own.

But the road wasn't smooth.

For years, big companies told him he didn't have enough experience or enough skills. Doors closed before he could even prove himself. Instead of giving up, he took roles with smaller companies — places willing to give him a shot. He built his skills, earned his certifications, and let his work speak for him.

Then he circled back to those same big companies.

This time, they didn't just open the door — they paid him what he was worth.

One of his proudest milestones was earning certifications like Security+, Cloud+, and CCNA. Coming from the medical field, those weren't just credentials. They were proof — proof that he belonged, proof that he could learn a new language, proof that he could build a new life.

Passing the Torch — Denzell's Wisdom

"Your path doesn't have to be straight for you to win.
You're allowed to start over.
You're allowed to grow.

Don't let fear talk you out of your future."

SECTION III – RESILIENCE & REINVENTION

DEVIN – Product Manager • Builder at Heart • Champion for Representation in Tech

Impact: *From startups to Excel AI – building features that millions use and mentoring the next generation to see themselves in tech.*

Devin's journey into technology didn't begin with a childhood full of gadgets or a family legacy in engineering. He grew up in Vallejo, California – a place where the paths that seemed most visible were sports or music. Tech wasn't something people around him talked about. It didn't feel like a realistic future.

He went to college to play football and started out studying biochemistry, imagining a career in medicine. But everything shifted the day he took an introductory engineering class. For the first time, someone explained what engineering actually is – the art of building things that people use, love, and rely on. That single moment lit a spark that changed the direction of his life.

He switched majors, leaned into his curiosity, and discovered that he loved creating products from scratch. Before joining Microsoft, he founded two startups, learning firsthand what it means to build with limited resources, talk to users, iterate fast, and solve real problems. Those experiences sharpened his instincts and shaped the product manager he would eventually become.

Today, Devin is a Product Manager at Microsoft, working on Excel AI – one of the most widely used tools in the world. He builds features that help millions of people work smarter, faster, and more creatively. But for all the impact of his work, the most rewarding part of his journey is something deeper: giving back.

He cares deeply about helping people who look like him see that tech is not only possible — it's accessible. He knows what it feels like to be the first, the only, or the one who isn't sure they belong. And he knows how powerful it is to have someone reach back and say, "You can do this too."

His path hasn't been easy. Breaking into the industry, learning to navigate corporate dynamics, and growing into the responsibilities of a strong PM all came with challenges. But Devin learned to rely on people — mentors who gave honest feedback, peers who modeled excellence, and leaders who helped him think longterm. He studies the best around him and applies those lessons with intention.

Devin speaks openly about how Dwight's mentorship shaped his mindset, especially during the hard days. Reading Dwight's book, absorbing his "Dwightisms," and learning how you navigate growth as a person of color gave him a framework for consistency, resilience, and purpose. Devin credits Dwight's guidance for helping him earn two promotions in 18 months — a milestone he carries with pride.

One of Devin's proudest accomplishments is building and launching multiple companies. Starting something from nothing forces you to learn quickly, adapt constantly, and trust your instincts. It taught him how to build products people actually want — a skill that continues to shape his work today.

Passing the Torch — Devin's Wisdom

"Keep going.
Your journey is a marathon.
Start where you are, stay consistent, and let your work reflect your passion."

TIM — Military Leader • Information Security Professional • Voice of Resilience and Representation

Impact: *Two decades of service and a master's in InfoSec; orchestrates teams with the discipline and rhythm of a bandleader.*

Tim has spent nearly two decades serving in the military, bringing dedication, discipline, and a sharp sense of humor to every environment he steps into. Alongside his service, he built a career in technology rooted in curiosity — the kind of curiosity that makes a person ask not just what something does, but why and how it works. To Tim, technology isn't just a system — it's a rhythm. Like music, it has patterns, structure, and the power to transform lives when orchestrated well.

Originally from Florida, Tim grew up loving sports and carrying a natural drive to understand the mechanics behind everything around him. That instinct eventually led him to pursue a master's degree in Information Security, deepening his technical foundation and expanding the impact he could make both inside and outside the military.

For Tim, the most rewarding part of his journey has been representation. He's crossed paths with younger and older minorities who see his consistency, his attitude, and his resilience — and feel encouraged by it. He knows firsthand how powerful it is to see someone who looks like you thriving in spaces where you're not always expected. His presence becomes a reminder that possibility is real.

But his path hasn't been without challenges.

In the military and similar environments, Tim has faced prejudice and assumptions when stepping into leadership roles. He's had to navigate moments where people underestimated him before they understood him. Instead of letting those experiences harden him, he learned to maintain a strong mind and stay focused on growth. He reminds himself — and others — that until you've met the whole world, you can't let a few voices define what unity can achieve.

His advice to the next generation is poetic and powerful:

Your story matters.
Tech has its own rhythm — many can listen, but only some will orchestrate.
Be the one who orchestrates.

He encourages young technologists to stay curious, stay resilient, and trust that they belong in every room they walk into. Challenges are temporary. Impact is lasting.

One of his proudest milestones is becoming the first in his family to achieve this level of consistency in a military career, earn a master's degree in Information Security, and travel the world. It's proof that perseverance and passion can break generational barriers and create new paths.

Passing the Torch — Tim's Wisdom

"Your story matters.
Be the one who orchestrates.
Challenges are temporary — your impact can be lasting."

MISRAK — Senior Data Engineer • Global Thinker • Proof That Big Dreams Grow in Small Places

Impact: *From solving a trafficlight problem without ever seeing one to designing global data systems that move insight at scale.*

Misrak's story begins in a small village in western Ethiopia — a place where Western technology felt distant, almost abstract. Yet even there, her curiosity was alive. In eighth grade, she found herself solving a physics problem about a traffic light, despite never having seen one in real life. That moment — imagining a system she had never encountered — revealed something important: education could connect imagination to reality. It was her first glimpse of what technology could make possible.

That spark grew into a love for mathematics and problemsolving, eventually leading her to become one of only three women to graduate with a mathematics degree from Addis Ababa University. From there, she pursued a Master's degree in Computer Science in the United States — a leap that required courage, resilience, and a belief that her dreams were worth chasing.

Today, Misrak is a senior data engineer, designing and working with data systems at a global scale. Her work shapes how information flows, how systems learn, and how organizations make decisions. But her journey is about far more than technical skill — it's about possibility.

The most rewarding part of her path has been seeing how determination transformed dreams that once felt impossibly distant into reality. She knows what it means to be the only Black woman in the room — to question her voice, soften her accent, or hesitate to speak up. She knows the weight of visibility and the temptation to shrink.

But she also knows the power of perseverance.

Over time, she learned to take up space, trust her voice, and recognize that belonging does not require assimilation. Her perspective has value. Her background is a strength. And her presence is a reminder that brilliance comes from everywhere — even the places the world overlooks.

Passing the Torch — Misrak's Wisdom

"Obstacles do not define you — persistence does. Your background is a source of strength, not a limitation. Keep going, even when the dream feels distant."

SHUNDRELL — Business Program Manager • Culture Builder • Architect of Confidence and Belonging

Impact: *Designs the operating rhythm for teams and builds learning and recognition programs that make belonging tangible.*

Shundrell guides the heartbeat of how her organization operates. As a business program manager, she shapes the planning rhythms, reviews, and communications that keep teams aligned and moving forward. She also leads employee recognition and learning programs — work that cultivates a culture where people feel seen, valued, and inspired to grow. Her impact isn't measured in code or architecture, but in the systems of people, trust, and belonging that make great work possible.

Her path into tech wasn't linear. She once dreamed of becoming a TV correspondent, imagining a life in broadcasting. Later, she explored government work and even held roles in both fields. But life shifted — motherhood, relocation, and changing circumstances pulled her in new directions. When her husband was recruited by a technology company, she found herself in a new city, surrounded by a new industry. She didn't arrive with a spark for tech — she arrived with openness.

"When in Rome," she told herself.

That simple decision opened the door to the career she has today.

The most rewarding part of her journey has been discovering that she belongs in a technology company even without a technical background. She found an environment where the sky truly is the limit — where she can learn, explore, and train on any technology that sparks her curiosity. And in this new era of AI, she has found unexpected joy in building AIdriven solutions that make her work easier and more efficient. She didn't expect to love creating tools with AI, but now she's energized by what she can design, automate, and imagine.

But her path has not been without challenges.

Shundrell has faced the realities many women — especially Black women — know well: tribalism, unconscious bias, mansplaining, and the weight of the "Black tax." Yet she's honest about something many people don't say out loud:

the biggest barriers weren't always external — they were internal.

She spent years believing she had to be perfect before taking the next step. She replayed conversations, secondguessed herself, and wondered how others perceived her. Even when she knew she was capable, she battled the quiet voice that asked whether she truly belonged.

Over time, she learned that growth isn't just about overcoming the biases around us — it's about confronting the ones we carry within ourselves. Every day, she rewrites that inner dialogue with confidence, clarity, and courage.

Her advice to the next generation is direct and liberating:

Go for it.
Prepare yourself, do the work, stay committed to learning — but don't wait until you feel perfect to move.
Never let anyone else define who you are or what you're capable of. Only God has that authority.

A mantra her husband shared with their family has stayed with her:

Success = Attitude × Effort.

Your mindset and your willingness to show up will always carry you farther than fear.

One of the most meaningful milestones in her journey came from an unexpected place — her partnership with her husband. For years, she saw herself as the woman behind the man, cheering him on, encouraging him, offering sparks that often became the seeds of his breakthroughs. What she didn't realize was that his passion for technology — and his belief that anyone can learn it — was quietly shaping her path too.

She may have stood behind him at times, but he also stood beside her — opening doors, pulling her forward, and helping her discover a technical journey she never expected to have.

That shift — from quietly supporting someone else's path to boldly stepping into her own — is one of the most significant milestones of her career.

Passing the Torch — Shundrell's Wisdom

"Go for it.
Don't wait to feel perfect before you move.
Your attitude and your effort will carry you farther than fear."

SECTION IV – THE FUTURE

RODAS – Quality Assurance Intern • Rising Technologist • Voice of Representation and Resilience

Impact: *Year Up to Microsoft QA; balances a UW Informatics degree ('27) while testing for reliability and inclusion.*

Rodas is early in her journey, but she carries herself with the clarity, discipline, and quiet strength of someone who already understands the weight of her presence. Originally from Ethiopia, she is building her foundation as a Quality Assurance intern at Microsoft, supporting product quality, testing, and validation to ensure technology is reliable, inclusive, and ready for the world.

Alongside her internship, she is pursuing a Bachelor's degree in Informatics at the University of Washington, graduating in 2027. Her academic and professional paths are unfolding in parallel – each reinforcing the other, each shaping her into the technologist she is becoming.

Her path into tech wasn't a straight line. Before joining Year Up United, she was studying Computer Science, slowly discovering her place in the field. She had curiosity, she had drive, but she also had doubt. She wasn't always sure she could compete for internships or break into the industry. She wasn't always sure she belonged.

Year Up became the bridge.

It arrived at a moment when she needed a push – a reminder that the work she had already been doing mattered. She took a chance on herself, applied, and was accepted. That decision changed everything. It connected her academic journey to realworld opportunity and ultimately led her to Microsoft.

For Rodas, the most rewarding part of her journey has been representation. Being both Black and a woman in tech carries a unique kind of power. Every step she takes forward expands what's possible for someone watching. Seeing other Black women thrive, lead, and show up confidently in tech reminds her that she is not an anomaly — she is part of a lineage of changemakers. And knowing that her presence alone might inspire someone else to believe they belong is deeply meaningful to her.

But her journey hasn't been without challenges.

One of the hardest parts has been navigating the uncertainty of being an intern working toward a fulltime role. She has done all the "right things" — networking, meeting recruiters, talking to HR, applying consistently — and still learned that results don't always come immediately. She has applied to many opportunities knowing that only one "yes" is needed.

What helps her navigate this season is faith. She believes in trusting God's timing, understanding that effort does not always equal immediate results — but it is never wasted. She moves forward with confidence, patience, and the belief that what is meant for her will come at the right time.

Her advice to others is simple and powerful:

"You are here for a reason.
If you didn't belong, you wouldn't be in the room."

She knows imposter syndrome is real. She knows there will be moments where you feel unsure, invisible, or discouraged. But she also knows that your presence alone means you earned your place. She encourages others to fight for what they want, stay consistent, and refuse to give up just because the journey feels hard.

Mentorship has played a major role in shaping her mindset. Through Microsoft, she has had meaningful conversations with mentors — including Mildred Jammer — who offered guidance that stayed with her. One piece of advice she carries with her is:

"Not every piece of feedback is meant to be taken inside — you can hear it without absorbing it."

That wisdom helped her protect her confidence, her identity, and her sense of belonging.

One of her proudest milestones is earning her Microsoft internship through Year Up United. It represents resilience, growth, and proof that nontraditional paths into tech are valid and powerful. Balancing a demanding internship while pursuing her degree has shown her what she is capable of — and motivates her to aim even higher.

Rodas is still writing her story, but she already understands something many people take years to learn:

faith, patience, and persistence matter.
Growth often happens quietly before it becomes visible.

Passing the Torch — Rodas' Wisdom

"You are here for a reason.
If you didn't belong, you wouldn't be in the room.
Choose faith over fear, stay consistent, and trust the timing."

Closing — Passing the Torch to You

The pattern is plain: the torch is not a metaphor we admire; it is a tool we use. These builders faced bias, ceilings, and silence — and then punctured all three with delivery, mentorship, and faith. They did not wait for rooms to change. They changed rooms.

If God be for you, who can be against you.

That is the truth I carry as I close this chapter, and the truth I pray you carry into your own journey. These fifteen stories reveal something the world has tried to hide from us: that Black people were made to advance technology, that our brilliance has always been the engine of innovation, and that our worth has never depended on recognition.

My hope is that these voices awaken something in you — a knowing, a confidence, a calling. We have a responsibility now: to lead in the age of AI, to raise our hands when we see underrepresentation, to ensure our lens is present in the data that will shape the future, and to come together as one people across continents and cultures.

I write these books to close the digital divide, to reach the underrepresented, to build pathways for those searching for a way forward. And if this were my final message to you, I would want you to remember this:

We are all created in the image of God.
Love Him.
Love your neighbor.
Stand for peace, love, and justice.
Do what is right.
Leave no one behind.
And allow God to use you for a purpose greater than yourself.

The torch is in your hands now — carry it farther than we ever dreamed.

ACKNOWLEDGMENTS

To my wife and children — thank you for being my foundation, my inspiration, and my greatest joy. To every mentor, colleague, and student who walked this journey with me — your belief fueled my purpose. To the pioneers whose shoulders I stand on — your brilliance lights the way. And to every reader who sees themselves in these pages — may this book remind you that you are not alone, and that your story matters.

Special thanks to the fifteen colleagues, friends, and family who courageously shared their stories in this book: **Dave, Devin, Michael, Yinka, Rodas, Tim, Robert, Misrak, Shundrell, Dion, Kelechi, Musa, Austin, Nafiva, and Denzell.** I believe your stories and testimonies will pave the way for the next generation.

Images of Dwight as a speaker and author

ABOUT THE AUTHOR

Dwight D. Jones Sr.

Veteran technologist • Author • Speaker • Mentor

Dwight D. Jones Sr. is a veteran technologist, author, speaker, and mentor with four decades of experience leading digital transformation across multiple industries. From his early days working third shift in a mainframe data center to helping support and build Microsoft's Windows and cloud infrastructure – and later launching Skype for Business and Microsoft Teams – Dwight has lived through every major wave of modern computing.

A passionate advocate for equity in tech, he has mentored thousands of underrepresented technologists and built programs that opened doors for the next generation. His journey is rooted in resilience, faith, and purpose, and his mission is unwavering: to ensure that Black excellence is not only remembered, but recognized, celebrated, and empowered to lead the future.

Dwight also carries a rare and profound connection to American history. As part of the final generation who can say they have personally touched every stage of the digital divide, he also treasures the memory of knowing his grandfather – born in 1871 on the Jones slave plantation in Stanton, Virginia. To live a life that spans from knowing a grandfather born into slavery to contributing to the world's leading technology company is a story worth sharing.

Dwight is grateful for every pivot, every challenge, and every breakthrough that shaped his remarkable journey.

From humble beginnings to a legacy builder & force multiplier.

Images of Dwight speaking and engaging the community

Dwight continues to build, lead, and grow as a lifelong learner, technologist, speaker, and author.

Images of Dwight's career as a technologist, speaker, author, and learner

What Dwight Is Most Proud Of

More than titles, awards, or accomplishments, Dwight is most proud of:

- His journey from humble beginnings
- His contributions to the world through technology
- The legacy he has built
- His life's purpose to pay it forward by lifting up everyone he meets

Collage of Dwight and contributors to his purpose and legacy

Advocacy for the Next Generation – In Action

To book Dwight for your next community outreach, education, or corporate event, reach out via LinkedIn. Books available on Amazon.

Images of The Yahweh Group, LLC – Dwight's platform for speaking engagements, books, and educational content.
Book Dwight for speaking, coaching, and booksigning events.
Connect on LinkedIn.

THE YAHWEH
GROUP, LLC

www.ingramcontent.com/pod-product-compliance
Lightning Source LLC
LaVergne TN
LVHW022228200926
848481LV00006B/2177
* 9 7 9 8 2 3 4 0 2 0 5 8 1 *